DATE DUE

~~DE 22 '95~~			
~~DE 18 '96~~			
			JUL '90

DEMCO 25-380

JACK
JOHNSON

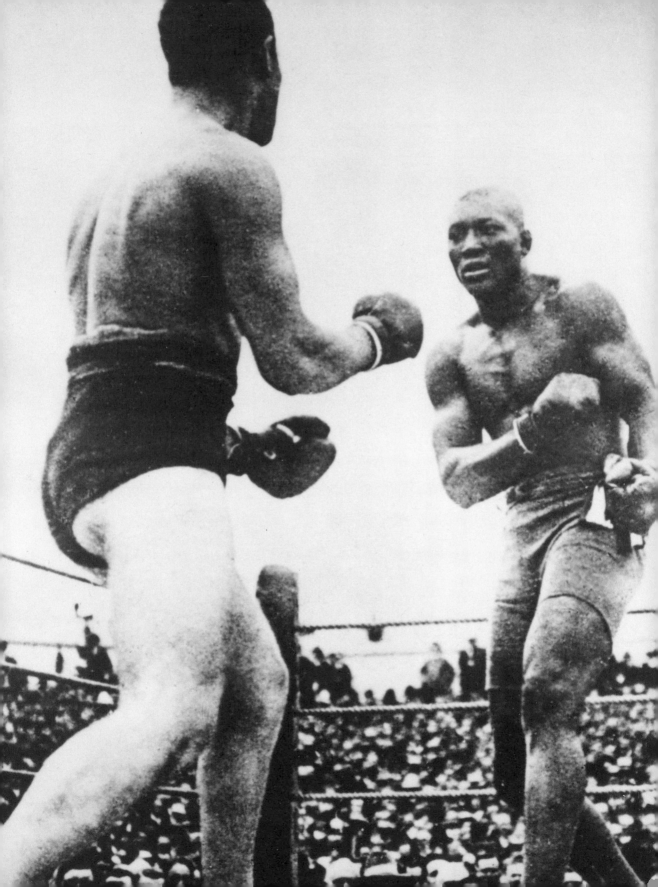

JACK JOHNSON

◄☙►

Robert Jakoubek

Senior Consulting Editor
Nathan Irvin Huggins
Director
W.E.B. Du Bois Institute for Afro-American Research
Harvard University

CHELSEA HOUSE PUBLISHERS
New York   Philadelphia

Chelsea House Publishers
Editor-in-Chief   Remmel Nunn
Managing Editor   Karyn Gullen Browne
Copy Chief   Juliann Barbato
Picture Editor   Adrian G. Allen
Art Director   Maria Epes
Deputy Copy Chief   Mark Rifkin
Assistant Art Director   Loraine Machlin
Manufacturing Manager   Gerald Levine
Systems Manager   Rachel Vigier
Production Manager   Joseph Romano
Production Coordinator   Marie Claire Cebrián

Black Americans of Achievement
Senior Editor   Richard Rennert

Staff for JACK JOHNSON
Editorial Assistant   Leigh Hope Wood
Picture Researcher   Alan Gottlieb
Designer   Ghila Krajzman
Cover Illustration   Alan J. Nahigian

First Printing

1 3 5 7 9 8 6 4 2

Library of Congress Cataloging-in-Publication Data

Jakoubek, Robert E.
    Jack Johnson, heavyweight champion/by Robert Jakoubek.
        p.   cm.—(Black Americans of achievement)
    Includes bibliographical references.
    Summary: Describes the life of the black who won the heavyweight
championship boxing title in 1908.
    ISBN 0-7910-1113-5
          0-7910-1139-9 (pbk.)
    1. Johnson, Jack, 1878–1946.   2. Boxers (Sports)—United
States—Biography.   [1. Johnson, Jack, 1878–1946.   2. Boxers
(Sports) 3. Afro-Americans—Biography.]   I. Title.   II. Series.
GV1132.J7J35 1990   90-31818
796.8'3'092—dc20   CIP
[B]   AC

*Frontispiece: Jack Johnson
(right) battles Tommy Burns for
the world heavyweight championship on December 26, 1908.*

CONTENTS

———— ❦ ————

BLACK
AMERICANS
OF
ACHIEVEMENT

Muhammad Ali
heavyweight champion

Richard Allen
*founder of the
African Methodist
Episcopal church*

Louis Armstrong
musician

James Baldwin
author

Benjamin Banneker
*scientist and
mathematician*

Mary McLeod Bethune
educator

Blanche K. Bruce
politician

Ralph Bunche
diplomat

George Washington Carver
botanist

Charles Waddell Chestnutt
author

Paul Cuffe
merchant and abolitionist

Frederick Douglass
abolitionist editor

Charles R. Drew
physician

W.E.B. Du Bois
scholar and activist

Paul Laurence Dunbar
poet

Duke Ellington
bandleader and composer

Ralph Ellison
author

Ella Fitzgerald
singer

Marcus Garvey
black-nationalist leader

Prince Hall
social reformer

William H. Hastie
educator and politician

Matthew A. Henson
explorer

Chester Himes
author

Billie Holiday
singer

John Hope
educator

Lena Horne
entertainer

Langston Hughes
poet

James Weldon Johnson
author

Scott Joplin
composer

Martin Luther King, Jr.
civil rights leader

Joe Louis
heavyweight champion

Malcolm X
militant black leader

Thurgood Marshall
Supreme Court justice

Elijah Muhammad
religious leader

Jesse Owens
champion athlete

Gordon Parks
photographer

Sidney Poitier
actor

Adam Clayton Powell, Jr.
political leader

A. Philip Randolph
labor leader

Paul Robeson
singer and actor

Jackie Robinson
baseball great

John Russwurm
publisher

Sojourner Truth
antislavery activist

Harriet Tubman
antislavery activist

Nat Turner
slave revolt leader

Denmark Vesey
slave revolt leader

Madame C. J. Walker
entrepreneur

Booker T. Washington
educator

Walter White
political activist

Richard Wright
author

ON
ACHIEVEMENT

Coretta Scott King

BEFORE YOU BEGIN this book, I hope you will ask yourself what the word excellence means to you. I think that it's a question we should all ask, and keep asking as we grow older and change. Because the truest answer to it should never change. When you think of excellence, perhaps you think of success at work; or of becoming wealthy; or meeting the right person, getting married, and having a good family life.

Those important goals are worth striving for, but there is a better way to look at excellence. As Martin Luther King, Jr., said in one of his last sermons, "I want you to be first in love. I want you to be first in moral excellence. I want you to be first in generosity. If you want to be important, wonderful. If you want to be great, wonderful. But recognize that he who is greatest among you shall be your servant."

My husband, Martin Luther King, Jr., knew that the true meaning of achievement is service. When I met him, in 1952, he was already ordained as a Baptist preacher and was working towards a doctoral degree at Boston University. I was studying at the New England Conservatory and dreamed of accomplishments in music. We married a year later, and after I graduated the following year we moved to Montgomery, Alabama. We didn't know it then, but our notions of achievement were about to undergo a dramatic change.

You may have read or heard about what happened next. What began with the boycott of a local bus line grew into a national movement, and by the time he was assassinated in 1968 my husband had fashioned a black movement powerful enough to shatter forever the practice of racial segregation. What you may not have read about is where he got his method for resisting injustice without compromising his religious beliefs.

He adopted the strategy of nonviolence from a man of a different race, who lived in a distant country, and even practiced a different religion. The man was Mahatma Gandhi, the great leader of India, who devoted his life to serving humanity in the spirit of love and nonviolence. It was in these principles that Martin discovered his method for social reform. More than anything else, those two principles were the key to his achievements.

This book is about black Americans who served society through the excellence of their achievements. It forms a part of the rich history of black men and women in America—a history of stunning accomplishments in every field of human endeavor, from literature and art to science, industry, education, diplomacy, athletics, jurisprudence, even polar exploration.

Not all of the people in this history had the same ideals, but I think you will find something that all of them have in common. Like Martin Luther King, Jr., they all decided to become "drum majors" and serve humanity. In that principle—whether it was expressed in books, inventions, or song—they found something outside themselves to use as a goal and a guide. Something that showed them a way to serve others, instead of living only for themselves.

Reading the stories of these courageous men and women not only helps us discover the principles that we will use to guide our own lives but also teaches us about our black heritage and about America itself. It is crucial for us to know the heroes and heroines of our history and to realize that the price we paid in our struggle for equality in America was dear. But we must also understand that we have gotten as far as we have partly because America's democratic system and ideals made it possible.

We are still struggling with racism and prejudice. But the great men and women in this series are a tribute to the spirit of our democratic ideals and the system in which they have flourished. And that makes their stories special and worth knowing. ❦

JACK
JOHNSON

1

TIMES SQUARE

I N THE 1930s, Times Square may well have been the brightest spot on earth. At night, said a guidebook to New York, the midtown district's enormous electric signs gave off a "glow like that of a dry timber fire." In every direction, there blazed "a wall of light and color urging the onlooker to chew gum, drink beer, see the world's most beautiful girls." Lost in all the brilliance was a painted sign hanging over the entrance to a dreary amusement arcade along Broadway. It read: Jack Johnson Trains Here.

It cost a dime to go in and a dime to operate the game machines and moviolas that lined the walls. Toward the rear of the arcade, at the end of the narrow corridor between the machines, a space had been cleared, a record player set up, and a punching ball suspended from the ceiling. Punching the ball in time to the jazz tunes coming from the phonograph, stripped to the waist, wearing boxing tights and high-topped boxing shoes was the former heavyweight champion of the world, Jack Johnson.

New York City's glittering Times Square made an appropriate stomping ground for Johnson in the 1930s and 1940s, more than a quarter century after the flamboyant (and, according to some, morally bankrupt) fighter became the first black to win the world heavyweight title. During these two decades, he lectured on life's many lessons in Hubert's Museum, a sordid amusement arcade wedged between the bustling area's theaters and shops.

Candid shots of Johnson during an interview in April 1936. "My life, almost from its very start," he wrote in his autobiography, "has been filled with tragedy and romance, failure and success, poverty and wealth, misery and happiness. All these conflicting conditions that have crowded in upon me and plunged me into struggles with warring forces have made me somewhat of a unique character."

He was nearly 60, but nothing about him looked old. The muscles in Johnson's arms and legs still bulged, and he never missed a beat nor seemed to draw a deep breath as he punched effortlessly at the ball. His head, as always, was clean shaven, and it reflected the lights inside the arcade. Whenever a customer paused to say hello or ask something of him, Johnson would stop his workout, pull off a glove to shake hands, and then—to strangers and old friends alike—he would flash his famous, unforgettable trademark: the golden smile.

Each day in his little makeshift gym, Johnson happily sold copies of his out-of-print autobiography for a dollar apiece. For another dollar, he inscribed and signed the book. "Every word is true," he would say, slapping the book's cover. "It says so on the back."

Johnson was also glad to make change for the customers and direct them toward the arcade's movie machines. To drum up business, after all, was why he was there. Several machines featured films of his fights, and with enough time and enough dimes anyone who wished to relive the glory days of Jack Johnson could do so.

As the films threaded their way through the machines, the blurry old silent movies flickered and jerked. Nevertheless, the greatness of Jack Johnson came across as plain as day. He glided about the ring. His opponents, flailing away madly, could not harm him. He caught their blows with his gloves, with his elbows, with his biceps. He toyed arrogantly with his foes, letting round after round pass until, in a flash, his smile vanished and his fists went to work; he showed no mercy. The films almost always ended with a triumphant Johnson smiling his bright, broad golden smile.

For those who watched the films, there was no mistaking something else: Jack Johnson was black, and his opponents were white.

In 1935, a boxing enthusiast from England happened by the arcade, and throughout the next week he pushed a small fortune in dimes into the moviolas. Over and over, he watched the filmed image of Johnson beating Tommy Burns for the heavyweight title in 1908; of him battering Fireman Flynn and Stanley Ketchel; of the champion going 20 rounds with Frank Moran at the Vélodrome d'Hiver in Paris; of him humiliating the great James J. Jeffries on Independence Day, 1910, in Reno, Nevada; of his controversial loss to Jess Willard in 1915. And, amazingly, the hero of these fights was but five feet away, hammering away at a punch ball.

As Johnson punched, he talked, giving his English admirer a running commentary: "It was a big shame the way I treated Burns. I could have beaten Jeff any round I liked. I let Ketchel knock me down to make the movie more exciting. I only fought Flynn to please [fight promoter Jack] Curley. Moran and me never got a cent out of those twenty rounds in Paris. You know I laid down for Willard so that I could come home and see my mother. They treated me bad, man, but I got the better of them."

Johnson was never at a loss for words. He loved talking about his years as champion and delighted in comparing current fighters to himself. Invariably, the comparisons favored the old champion. During the mid-1930s, the hottest thing around was Joe Louis, the magnificent fighter from Detroit, who was destined to become the first black since Johnson to wear the heavyweight crown. When his English admirer at the arcade asked jokingly for whom he was training, Johnson snapped, "That Louis boy, of course. If they'll let me, I'll give him a boxing lesson over three rounds. That Joe has a lot to learn." Long after Louis had shown he had next to nothing to learn, Johnson continued to ridicule him.

That was how it had always been. Johnson seldom gave other black fighters the time of day. He craved the spotlight and resisted sharing it. When people thought of a black champion, he wanted the name Jack Johnson and none other to spring to mind.

But by the 1930s, Johnson's wish amounted to a pipe dream. He had come to be regarded as a forlorn, even pathetic figure. The black fighters, like Louis, who might have honored his accomplishments and hailed him as a pioneer in black athletics steered clear of him. Their managers, trainers, and promoters seldom let a day go by without reminding them, "Don't be another Jack Johnson," which was another way of saying, "Don't get the whites mad."

In Johnson's heyday, white America's widespread resentment of a black champion had exploded into such a howling hysteria that a Chicago newspaper reported it had become dangerous for Johnson to walk the streets. The champion had provoked this state of affairs by being himself—by doing the things whites denied blacks and by doing them openly, with proud defiance. He taunted and belittled his white opponents. He romanced and married white women. He drank champagne through a straw and owned a saloon with solid silver cuspidors. He smoked his cigars in a long gold holder and wore shoes of doeskin and crocodile leather.

Johnson had not gotten away with it. He eventually lost both his title and his freedom. In a particularly vindictive move, the federal government imprisoned him for 10 months at the Fort Leavenworth Penitentiary for an alleged violation of the Mann Act, the federal antiprostitution law. And by the 1930s, he had become a sideshow act at a Broadway arcade. No wonder ambitious fight managers begged their young black boxers not to become another Jack Johnson.

In 1936, Johnson began to appear at another Times Square location, Professor Hubert's Museum at 228 West 42nd Street. Years earlier, the building

had housed Murray's Roman Gardens, a restaurant advertising exotic decor and a revolving dance floor. Alcoholic stimulation of some sort was evidently needed to properly enjoy these attractions, because in 1920, with the beginning of Prohibition, the restaurant folded. Professor Hubert subsequently moved in his remarkable exhibits. There was a bearded lady; a human skeleton; a troupe of dancing midgets; Professor Renato, the sword swallower; the Wild Man from Borneo; Madam Catalina, the snake charmer; and, at regular intervals, performances by Professor Heckler's Flea Circus.

For a few weeks several times a year, Johnson appeared in the museum's basement. He no longer pretended to be in training. He merely sat on a three-foot platform and told stories.

Johnson savors a sweet moment in his heyday as a flattened Stanley Ketchel is counted out in the 12th round of their October 16, 1909, fight for the heavyweight title.

Johnson dressed in flashy, well-tailored suits, usually complemented by spats and wide red ties. On his head was a blue beret, and his right hand held a silver-headed walking stick that he tapped when he wanted to emphasize some point in a story. He had nothing in common with the nearby snake charmers and sword swallowers. To the writer John Lardner, who came by often, "he was dignified, aloof, and untouched by his surroundings." Johnson still spoke with a soft English accent, something he had picked up years earlier from his friend and partner, the West

Johnson's passion for driving fancy cars (usually at high speeds) added to his reputation as a fun-loving, freewheeling dandy. His high style of living also enraged many white Americans because Johnson's behavior did not fit their stereotype of a humble, obedient black.

Indian fighter Joe Walcott, and had refined during the years he had lived in London.

Johnson's specialty at Professor Hubert's Museum was answering questions. But no matter what anyone in the basement asked him, he immediately launched into his favorite subject—himself.

The stories he told! There were tales of him fighting off a 23-foot shark with nothing more than the sponge nets in his little sailboat, of him running after a kangaroo at such a clip that the poor animal dropped dead, of his being tempted by (but finally resisting) a German spy during the First World War, of his spectacular career as a matador in the bullfighting ring at Barcelona.

A few people who wandered into Hubert's museum scoffed at Johnson and his stories. Bill Corum, a New York sportswriter, acknowledged that on the platform the old champion was pleasant and articulate. But Corum could not help sensing "a leering and egotistical quality about the way he answered my questions and [it] made me wonder when I left if I really believed anything he had said." Corum had to ask Johnson about "whether for a drink, a few dollars, or just a whim, he might not contradict himself the next day."

Of course Johnson would—he most always did. He had never been a stranger to fantasy. Now, in his old age, he kept alive his heroic visions by repeating, embellishing, and making up fantastic tales. No one who gathered about him in Hubert's basement and stood transfixed as he spun his yarns—save the occasional spoilsport like Corum—seemed to mind in the least.

Not all of Johnson's stories were cut from the same cloth. His prizefighting career had been such a sensational success that it required little exaggeration. As for his private life, he often answered questions about his personal relationships with disarming candor.

Johnson in the third year of his reign as the heavyweight champion, with Etta Terry Duryea, a member of his sizable entourage. "I didn't court white women because I thought I was too good for the others, like they said," Johnson later told the writer John Lardner at Hubert's Museum. "It was just that they always treated me better."

One of Johnson's best stories, repeated frequently, had to do with his being chased by a dirigible. During the First World War, he said, the crew of a German dirigible attacking London spotted him driving home and gave chase, the giant airship zigzagging crazily through the air until, just when the Germans had him lined up in the sights of their guns, he zoomed into the safety of his garage.

The story might not have been wholly farfetched. Even from a blimp there would have been no problem identifying Johnson's car. He raced about London in an enormous Benz convertible, all white, with leopard-skin upholstery and gold fittings. Nor was there the slightest doubt about his talent for coaxing speed from an automobile. In 1909, when the speed limit was 5 miles per hour, he had pushed his Thompson Flier to more than 70 while joyriding through San Francisco's Golden Gate Park. His fondest dream, Johnson once told a reporter, was to drive 200 miles per hour.

Cars were a very important part of the champion's life. Behind the wheel, he was free in a way he— and every other black of his generation—could be free nowhere else. Regardless of how hard times became for him or how badly he needed cash, he kept a fine car.

Johnson retained his sense of style to the very end. In 1946, when he completed the last of his engagements at Professor Hubert's Museum and was departing from New York for a series of shows with a Texas carnival, he stepped out of the tawdry museum on 42nd Street, walked to the curb, and opened the door of his green Lincoln Zephyr, the one with leather seats, white sidewalls, and a V-12 engine that purred, then roared. ◕

2
GALVESTON

JOHN ARTHUR JOHNSON, the future heavy-weight champion of the world, was born on March 31, 1878, in Galveston, Texas, then the largest city in the Lone Star State. Located on an island in the Gulf of Mexico, 24 miles offshore, Galveston owed its size and well-being to its magnificent harbor. During Jack Johnson's youth, the port of Galveston was the nation's second busiest, and among his earliest memories was the thrill of seeing the towering masts of great ships from South America, Europe, and the West Indies.

In the daytime, the Galveston harbor swarmed with activity. Under a broiling sun, stevedores loaded and unloaded the ships, pushing, lifting, and heaving cargoes of cotton, lumber, and cottonseed oil from the ships to the sprawling complex of warehouses that lined the wharves. It was dirty, backbreaking work, but it was steady and paid well, and because of that there was never a shortage of newcomers seeking positions as longshoremen, yardmen, cotton classers, screw men, and all the other occupations of a port.

A youthful Johnson (back row, third from right), in his hometown of Galveston, Texas, poses with some of his cronies—among them fellow fighter Joe Choynski (standing, second from left). "I took up boxing," Johnson stated, "not with any intention of engaging in it as a profession, but because it seemed necessary for me to learn something of the science in order to pit myself against the fighting groups with whom I associated."

The activity and prosperity of Galveston set it apart from the rest of the South. Defeat in the Civil War still hung over the region like a toxic, suffocating cloud. "Fifteen years have gone over the South," wrote a New York editor in 1879, "and she still sits crushed, wretched, busy displaying and bemoaning her wounds." Galveston was the exception, resembling a northern city in its optimism, in the feeling of its citizens that there was money to be made and that time was wasting.

Galveston held opportunity even for blacks. The docks were thoroughly integrated, and by 1877 black longshoremen were being paid the same as their fellow white workers, $2 a day. For the blacks of the post–Civil War South, $2 a day, or, for that matter, $1 a day or 50¢ a day was a small fortune. After all, they had been slaves less than a generation earlier.

Henry Johnson, Jack's father, had been born a slave on a Maryland plantation in 1838. By some accounts, as a young man he had entertained his masters in exhibitions of bare-knuckled boxing. Later, during the Civil War, he evidently served the Confederate army of General Robert E. Lee in some menial capacity. In the aftermath of war, lured by the promise of a better life, he had managed to find his way to Galveston.

To a certain extent, Henry Johnson found in Galveston what he had been looking for. An injury that had left him partly paralyzed ruled out work on the docks, but he found decent work as a woodworker, a saloon porter, and, finally, as a school janitor. He married a woman named Tiny, 19 years his junior, and with her settled down to a quiet family life. Together they raised six children, four daughters and two sons, of whom Jack was the eldest.

By the early 1880s, the Johnsons were living at 808 Broadway, in a one-story wooden house with a basement and enclosed porch that Henry Johnson had built himself. Henry and Tiny insisted their children be educated and pious and saw to their regular attendance at school and church. At home, Tiny, a small, round woman, ruled the roost, reaching for a switch or a two-by-four to restore order among the Johnson children.

Jack, she worried, was less a troublemaker than a coward. As a youngster, he was forever coming home bruised and bloody, crying that some neighborhood bully had beaten him up once more. Even Tiny had to admit he was a likely target. Tall and awkward, he often put on a dirty old apron and helped his father with his janitor's duties at school. His classmates loved nothing more than stopping by and taunting him as he pushed along his broom. They sensed his fear and knew he would not retaliate. Worse still, Jack always let one of his older sisters do his fighting for him. When they were not around, he just took his beating.

Tiny decided something had to be done. Motioning to her two-by-four, she informed Jack that if he did not start fighting back, he would get a beating from her worse than anything a local bully could hand out. Jack began fighting and, to his delight, discovered he was good at it. What he had was speed, and he was soon knocking his tormentors silly. "Jack was so fast he could block a punch and hit you with the same hand," an old Galveston friend recalled. Never again did Jack come home in tears.

Jack had no difficulty with school, learning reading and arithmetic with ease, but by the fifth or sixth grade he had had enough of it. Leaving school, he took the first job he found; for $1.25 a week, he helped deliver milk. Never one to keep at the same thing for long, he moved on to Gregory's Livery Stables, where, for about the same money, he walked horses. Fired for overexercising the animals, Jack for a time painted wagons and, after that, apprenticed

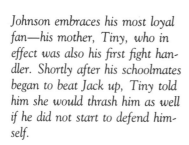

Johnson embraces his most loyal fan—his mother, Tiny, who in effect was also his first fight handler. Shortly after his schoolmates began to beat Jack up, Tiny told him she would thrash him as well if he did not start to defend himself.

in a bakery. Just when he mastered baking bread, he got bored with it and headed to the Galveston waterfront and a job unloading ships.

The docks were a long way from the bakery and stables. Jack described his fellow longshoremen as "some of the toughest and hardest-boiled men imaginable. To them, fighting was one of the important functions of existence. They fought on every occasion and on any pretext." Although still in his teens, Jack had grown into an imposing six-footer, and with his natural skill and speed he rudely thrashed the older roughnecks who had the bad luck to pick a fight with him.

He was different from his father. Year after year, Henry Johnson had labored for a small stake in life: a wife, a family, a little house—all that he had been denied in slavery. His son set his sights higher and in other directions. Jack idolized Steve Brodie, the New York saloonkeeper who in 1886 had leaped to fame and fortune by jumping off the Brooklyn Bridge. Not everyone was taken by the stunt—"Jumped off the bridge?" snorted the father of heavyweight boxer John L. Sullivan. "Any damn fool can do that. I thought he jumped *over* it"—but Jack dreamed of somehow matching Brodie's celebrity.

In the meantime, Jack drifted from job to job and place to place. In Galveston and in the little towns of south Texas, he worked, played, and fought with other young men. If he lost when they shot craps, he more than made up for it when they fought.

Inevitably, Jack got into the world of the battle royals, the "sport" of blacks beating one another up for the amusement of whites. In its most typical form, a battle royal involved eight or more blacks getting into a boxing ring and fighting until only one was left standing. The all-white audience hugely enjoyed the sight of the young blacks, sometimes tied together, sometimes blindfolded, swinging away. The victor was allowed to scoop up the nickels and pennies the spectators had tossed into the ring.

With his strength and talent, Jack usually came out on top; but of course in a battle royal there was no victor. The sordid affairs denigrated all the participants, winners and losers alike. The blacks in the ring were like so many pit bulls or fighting cocks. That was the whole point. Whites always boxed one-on-one, often with pride and gallantry. Only blacks, wildly swarming over one another, were denied any shred of dignity.

The miserable battle royals did not entirely spoil Jack's taste for fighting. On the wharves and in the alleys, he took on all challengers, and more and more often he began showing up at the private boxing clubs in and around Galveston. In these dim, smoky clubhouses, he sparred with other fighters, honed his skills, and fought his first professional matches. Gradually, he developed a distinctive style. He boxed not from a crouch but standing straight up, and he took great care with his footwork so as never to be off balance. A master at blocking an opponent's blows, he fought defensively, snapping stinging counterpunches at his foe's biceps and then, after several rounds, swiftly launching an offensive of his own. He already had as brutal a right uppercut as anyone in Galveston had seen, and when it landed with the power of his shoulders, back, and legs behind it, the fight was over.

Jack Johnson thought of himself as a professional fighter even if his victories in the boxing clubs earned him next to nothing. To pay his way, he continued to float between various jobs, among them barber's helper, dockhand, and porter. Nearing 20, he still lived at home with his parents, but he frequently crossed from Galveston to the mainland and hopped a passing freight train for some unknown destination. "Although I did not know where the train was bound for I was not greatly worried over the matter," he explained years later. "I did not know where I was going but I was on my way."

For several years, Johnson went on his way with Mary Austin, a light-skinned black girl from Galveston. "Mary was a splendid woman and I recall my life with her as one of the happiest periods of my existence," he said. Although they never married, he took to introducing her as "Mrs. Jack Johnson." After each excursion with Mary, he came home to Galveston, to his father's house at 808 Broadway, to another temporary job, and to more fights.

By the spring of 1899, Johnson figured he had whipped everyone worth fighting in Galveston and decided to try Chicago, the home of some of the best boxers in the business. In the big town, he hung out at various clubs and gyms, picking up work as a sparring partner and refining his talent in the process.

In May 1899, Johnson seemed to get a break when he was given a fight with John "Klondike" Haynes, a well-regarded black heavyweight who had won his nickname because he seemed to flourish in cold weather. But Johnson was in over his head. He held on through the first few rounds, but he could not keep the massive Klondike from boring in and drilling wicked shots to his body. After five rounds, bruised and exhausted, Johnson simply quit fighting and climbed out of the ring. Making matters worse, he blew his small purse at the racetrack. "I was not clever in picking winners and the proceeds of my first Chicago fight did me little good," he recalled. He retreated to Galveston.

A year after Johnson's return, on a late-summer weekend in 1900, Galveston became hell on earth. In the early-morning hours of Saturday, September 8, a hurricane of unimaginable force roared onto Galveston Island from the Gulf of Mexico. Winds of 120 miles per hour blew the buildings and houses of the city to pieces. Chunks of slate, bricks, stone, and mortar flew like shrapnel through the air, wounding and decapitating panic-stricken residents. Both the elaborate Victorian homes of the gentry and the miserable shacks of the poor collapsed during the onslaught. The relentless winds drove a tidal wave over the island, entirely flooding the city. It was the single worst natural catastrophe in American history; 6,000 helpless people perished.

"The conditions of thousands of those who have been spared is far more pitiable than that of the dead," wrote a reporter on the scene. "Their resources have been swept away by the wind and tide, and they are desolate in the midst of desolation." Insurrection and plunder followed the disaster. Thieves took to hacking off the ringed hands of the dead because the fingers were too swollen by water to allow for the jewelry to be easily removed.

A portrait of Mary Austin, a young black woman from Galveston with whom Johnson traveled for several years and referred to as his wife, although they were never officially married. After going together for a few years, the couple separated in Colorado in September 1902, right after Johnson beat Mexican Pete Everett in a 20-round bout.

One of the nation's top heavyweights at the turn of the century, veteran boxer Joe Choynski (opposite) played a central role in Johnson's development as a fighter. On February 25, 1901, Choynski fought Johnson in Galveston's Harmony Hall (right) and showed he was a much superior fighter, knocking Johnson out in the third round. The bout, which violated Texas's antiboxing law, subsequently landed them in the same jail cell, where Choynski became something of a mentor to Johnson and taught him how to block punches and use his footwork to fight defensively.

Henry Johnson's house, like nearly all the rest, was ruined. All that he had worked for was lost. Jack, by his own account, saved his father from the flood, then spent days feeding the hungry, caring for the sick, and burying the dead. Amid the destruction, the Johnson family separated for good.

Yet Jack stayed on in Galveston, probably because, even in the aftermath of the hurricane, boxing continued and there was a fighter in town he was aching to challenge: Joe Choynski, who for the past year had been employed as a trainer by the Galveston Athletic Club. In a long career as a heavyweight, he had battled nearly all the legendary champions, including John L. Sullivan, Bob Fitzsimmons, and Jim Jeffries, not beating them but always giving a good account of himself. If Johnson could handle Choynski, he would be well launched toward boxing success.

On February 25, 1901, they fought before a packed house in Galveston's Harmony Hall, a building, as a consequence of the hurricane, without a roof. Johnson proved no match for the veteran. In the third round, Choynski hit a right cross to the temple that sent Johnson sinking to the floor. He landed facedown and remained that way until the referee counted to 10.

The evening was not over.

As Johnson groggily staggered to his feet and Choynski clasped his hands over his head in triumph, five Texas Rangers stormed into the ring. They bellowed out orders from the governor of Texas that the two fighters were under arrest. The crowd jeered, but the rangers led a puzzled Choynski and a woozy Johnson out of the hall and across town to the municipal jail.

Prizefighting was illegal in Texas (as it was in most states), yet the law against it had seldom been enforced. But the frightful lawlessness that followed the hurricane had changed things. Governor Joseph Sayers was determined to clean up Galveston, and he, like nearly all reformers, held a decidedly low opinion of professional fighters and the company they kept.

Unable to meet their $5,000 bonds, Johnson and Choynski spent 24 days behind bars. At first, it was not so bad. The two were local celebrities, and they received gentle treatment. Stuck with the young fighter for a jailmate, Choynski opened up and talked and talked about boxing, in the process revealing countless tricks of his trade. Later on, Johnson would put these invaluable lessons to good use in the ring.

By the end of their third week together, they were getting a trifle tired of each other. At last, in March 1901, after their bail had been reduced and paid, they were set free.

"After this event," Johnson wrote, "Galveston held no great charm for me and I again set out for new fields." ❧

3

"I WILL NOT FIGHT A NEGRO"

IN THE FALL of 1901, Jack Johnson left Galveston for California. The Golden State's warm weather, along with its reputation as the boxing capital of the world, drew him west.

Johnson took with him a great talent. In Galveston, the savvy Joe Choynski had seen past Johnson's rough edges and sized him up as a fighter with a perfect stance, awesome power, quick reflexes, and a clever head—in short, everything a boxer could want. For all his gifts, though, Johnson's two big fights—against Klondike Haynes in Chicago and Choynski in Galveston—had been poor showings. The old pros had used a few of their tricks and feints, and the raw young novice had fallen for them. At the age of 23, he was still a very long way from the heavyweight championship.

Even if Johnson had trained and sparred and refined his natural skills until he was something resembling an unbeatable fighting machine, he still would have been miles from the championship. It was not a question of talent. It was a question of color.

A color line ran straight through boxing. Johnson had fought and sparred with a number of whites in Galveston and Chicago, but it was risky business. In 1897, a prizefight between a black and a white had been stopped in New Orleans. "The idea of niggers fighting white men," scoffed the official who had

"I had the dreams and desires that are common to youth," Johnson said, "but never in the wildest moments of my boyhood imagination did I vision myself the champion fighter of the world, and the first man of my race ever to attain that distinction."

broken the fight up. "Why, if that darned scoundrel would beat that white boy the niggers would never stop gloating over it, and, as it is, we have enough trouble with them."

This sort of feeling became more intense the closer one got to the championship. The first American heavyweight champion, John L. Sullivan, "the Boston Strongboy," had refused to defend his title against Peter Jackson, an outstanding black contender from the West Indies. "I will not fight a Negro," the champion proclaimed. "I never have and I never shall." Each of Sullivan's successors as champion—James J. Corbett, Robert Fitzsimmons, and James J. Jeffries—followed his lead and rejected bouts with blacks. The color line was drawn a little less firmly in the lighter weight divisions, and for a half-dozen years after the turn of the century two blacks, Joe Walcott and Joe Gans, reigned respectively as welterweight and lightweight champions.

But the handwriting was on the wall, in boxing and in American society as a whole. During the 1890s and early 1900s, segregation of the races emerged in full, unsightly flower. In the South, where nearly nine-tenths of America's blacks lived, any pretense of racial equality was buried. The southern states systematically denied blacks the right to vote, and in 1896 the Supreme Court of the United States, in the landmark case *Plessy v. Ferguson*, upheld the right of the states to impose segregation in public facilities.

Something amounting to an antiblack crusade went hand in hand with segregation. A good measure of the bitter racist attitudes of the time were the novels of Thomas Dixon, most particularly *Leopard's Spots* (1902) and *The Clansman* (1905). Avidly read by millions in the North and the South, the novels drew a particularly unfortunate picture of black men. On the outside, Dixon wrote, they were Sambos— lazy, shiftless, irresponsible, childish. According to

In 1882, John L. Sullivan became the first boxer to win the world heavyweight championship. Blacks were not granted a shot at the title for the next 25 years— until fight promoters, unable to come up with a viable white contender, allowed Johnson to battle for the crown.

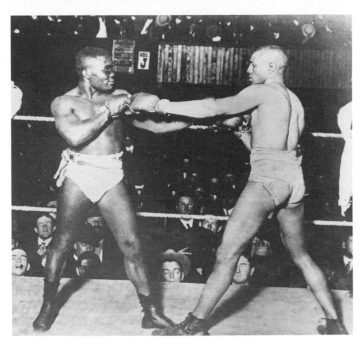

Lightweight titleholder Joe Gans (left) squares off against welter-weight champion Joe Walcott in 1904. They were among the few black boxers permitted by the sport's promoters to gain the top rank in the lighter-weight divisions.

Dixon, that was just a masquerade. Beneath the Sambo mask stirred a monster; the black male was a cunning animal lusting after white women and bent on orgies of rape and murder. Tragically, Dixon was merely preaching to the choir. With startling uni-formity, white America accepted as gospel these lies about blacks and viewed separation of the races as the only salvation.

In practical terms, the color line meant that Jack Johnson's chances of gaining the heavyweight cham-pionship were approximately zero. His boxing career, if he stayed with it and if he was lucky, would likely be a succession of fights with other blacks and third-rate whites. It would mean barnstorming the country, looking for whatever action he could find. But it also held the hope of handsome paydays, fleeting fame, and the chance to be a good distance from the drudg-ery of the Galveston wharves.

Just about what could be expected turned up for Johnson in California. In the desert town of Bakersfield, a gun-carrying saloon owner matched Johnson with Hank Griffin, a rugged, 6-foot-4-inch black heavyweight who possessed what was supposed to be the longest reach in boxing. Johnson went the distance, 20 rounds, holding his own but losing the decision. A few months later, the two battled once more, this time in Oakland. Johnson showed that he was improving; the rematch was a 15-round draw.

During the winter of 1902, fights proved hard to come by in California, and Johnson hit the road. In icy, wind-blasted Chicago, though bone tired from traveling halfway across the continent, he managed a six-round draw with Frank Childs, at the time one of the best black heavyweights in the country. During the next three months, Johnson stayed on the move, winding his way east to Philadelphia, then looping back toward California. Along the way, he won five fights, four by knockouts. His reputation was growing.

It had, in fact, grown large enough for him to breach the color line. On May 16, 1902, in Los Angeles, Johnson fought Jack Jeffries, the brother of the heavyweight champion. Jack bore his brother Jim not the slightest resemblance as a fighter, but because of his name people would always pay to see him fight, even if they usually got a mediocre show. The local newspapers made the most (or worst) of the black-white confrontation, one reporter describing Johnson as "a long, lean, bullet headed, flat-chested 'coon.' "

The bout got off to a slow start, the first few rounds boasting little activity. Johnson, as ever, fought defensively, gliding away from trouble and counterpunching when there was an opening. Suddenly, in the fifth round, like lightning from a cloudless sky, he unsheathed his right uppercut. Jeffries swooned to the canvas and, like that, the fight was over.

Johnson was giving the boxing world something to notice. As if his uppercut was not enough, his manner, his clothes, his style of life stopped nearly everyone in their tracks. For the Jack Jeffries fight, Johnson appeared wearing pink pajamas. And not just any pink, noted a reporter, but "one of those screaming, cater-wauling, belligerent pinks." Imagine the astonishment of the heavyweight champion Jim Jeffries, dressed in a dull gray sleeveless undershirt, as, from his seat at ringside, he sighted this black heavyweight in shocking pink saunter into the ring.

Away from the ring, whenever he could afford it, Johnson lived the high life. Endlessly attentive to his appearance, he always seemed to be adding to his wardrobe and always seemed to be changing clothes. One moment he might be in a golf cap and Norfolk jacket, the next in a dinner jacket. He ate well and drank with great good cheer. For one of his early

Johnson receives a speeding ticket from a Philadelphia policeman. An avid car fancier, the high-living boxer often showed a passion for fast driving.

fights, he bragged of training on a mixture of brandy and champagne.

As soon as Johnson had enough money, he bought a car—a shiny Winton—thereby becoming one of the first few thousand motorists in the United States. Driving became a lifelong passion. "I never had an ambition to be a real speed demon," he said, "but I must confess to have a weakness for fast driving." Over the years, he was hauled into court at least 20 times for traffic offenses, left in the dust Lord knows how many pursuing patrolmen, parked his car where he liked, and, for the fun of it, avoided the odd traffic jam by turning onto the sidewalk.

Following his win over Jack Jeffries, Johnson folded his many suits into his fine English luggage and again went on tour, knocking out his old nemesis Klondike Haynes in Memphis, then returning to California for a series of victories against some other black contenders. By the spring of 1903, he was in Philadelphia. In whatever town, east or west, Johnson trained at his own speed, sometimes seeming more concerned with entertaining the local blacks who showed up to watch him (and ignoring the whites) than in seriously preparing for his upcoming opponent. In the evenings, more times than not, he took his pleasure in a brothel.

It had been in a Philadelphia bar or brothel that Johnson had met Clara Kerr, a young black prostitute. "With Clara Kerr I became greatly infatuated," he recalled. "A deep attachment grew up between us which was to continue our association for a long time." For the next few years, they lived together in Philadelphia, Chicago, and California, Jack pursuing his profession and Clara hers. By Jack's account, Clara deserted him for an old friend of his, a horse trainer who, down on his luck, had moved in with them. Another version of their breakup has an unfaithful Jack leaving Clara. Whatever the truth, she was the last black woman with whom he lived. "The

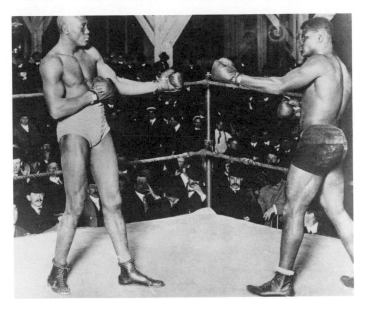

On February 27, 1903, Sam McVey (right), a powerfully built 17 year old, tried—without success—to win the Negro Heavyweight Championship that Johnson had captured on February 3 by defeating Denver Ed Martin. On October 27, McVey attempted once more to wrest the title from Johnson, but the result was exactly the same as their first meeting: a 20-round contest that culminated in a Johnson victory.

heartaches Mary Austin and Clara Kerr had caused me, led me to forswear colored women and to determine that my lot henceforth would be cast only with white women," he explained.

It was the most audacious judgment a black man of the early 1900s could make.

At the same time, Johnson's professional lot was being cast almost entirely with black fighters. Shunned by white professionals, the black heavyweights of the day developed their own circuit of competition. If anything, it was a finer brand of boxing than the all-white championships and included such powers as Denver Ed Martin, Sam McVey, Joe Jeannette, and Sam Langford.

By 1903, Johnson had emerged as the best of the lot. On February 3, in Los Angeles, he fought Denver Ed Martin, "the Colorado Giant," for the Negro Heavyweight Championship. Though still somewhat underweight at 180 pounds, Johnson struck with a fury in the 11th round, knocking down the much larger Martin 5 times. Denver Ed survived the storm, but Johnson easily won the 20-round fight on a decision.

Joe Jeannette (above) and Sam Langford (opposite) were among the top black boxers in the early 1900s. Johnson fought Jeannette a total of nine times (from 1905 to 1908) but battled Langford, who was widely regarded as Johnson's stiffest competition, only once (in 1906).

Less than a month later, Johnson defended his title against Sam McVey. Only 17, McVey was just beginning a career that would include, years later, an epic 49-round struggle against Joe Jeannette, in which the 2 fighters went down for the count a combined 46 times. At Hazard's Pavilion in Los Angeles on February 27, 1903, nothing so dramatic happened. For 20 rounds, Johnson toyed with the inexperienced McVey and won a victory by decision.

Seeking action, Johnson traveled all the time, sometimes with his good friend Joe Walcott, "the Barbados Demon," the welterweight champion of the world from 1901 until 1906. Only a half inch more than five feet, Walcott, in the phrase of the day, was a sawed-off Hercules. Absolutely fearless, often needing to jump up at his opponent to throw a punch, Walcott never let up during a fight and fired his fists from every possible angle. Over the years, he and Johnson sparred frequently, and once, on their way to Boston, the two were arrested for stealing a chicken. The little man's precise instruction helped Johnson polish his technique, and as if to show his gratitude, Johnson began affecting a British accent just like Walcott's.

On March 28, 1905, in San Francisco, Johnson broke out of the black ranks when he fought Marvin Hart, a leading white heavyweight from Kentucky. Hart had an eye on the heavyweight championship and knew that a victory over Johnson would help his reputation. A dedicated white supremacist, he also had a mind to teach Johnson a lesson. "Before the 20th round is reached—probably several rounds before—there'll be a nigger prostrate on the canvas," Hart predicted.

As he always did, Johnson started out cautiously, even passively, counterpunching when he had to, at other times moving away. Laughing and smiling, he seemed to be having a good time. Hart forced the action during the early rounds by awkwardly attempting to chase Johnson down. In the sixth round, Johnson took charge. His flashing jabs and counterpunches landed at will and raised mean-looking welts on Hart's face. In the 15th, Hart looked to be on his last legs. Purple bruises spotted his torso, and his nose and mouth were spurting blood. Yet he did not go down and, remarkably, appeared to recover. In the final rounds, he again pressed the action, and Johnson, looking a trifle tired, clinched and covered up.

When the fight ended after the 20th round, the decision was solely up to the referee, Alex Greggains. By the look of things, Johnson was the clear winner. He was virtually unmarked, whereas Hart was a bleeding mess. Greggains, however, had other ideas. He promptly proclaimed Hart the winner, later saying that Johnson had "dogged it" and "I always give the gamest and most aggressive man the decision." And, needless to say, the whitest. A bitter Johnson rightfully protested he had been "robbed."

Disgusted with California, Johnson moved east, for the next two years fighting mostly in Philadelphia. During this time, he faced a few white opponents, although never a top-notch contender. In July 1905, he squared off with Joe Grim, who, though technically white, was more often black and blue. "I am Joe Grim!" he liked to scream. "I fear no man on earth!" In his more than 300 fights, he had won 10, his talent consisting solely of a capacity to absorb bone-crushing punishment and then ask for more.

Johnson came within a few seconds of being the only man to knock Grim out. During their 6-round encounter, Johnson sent him crashing to the canvas 18 times. When the fight reached its last few seconds, Grim was down, nearly senseless, writhing in pain, and the referee was counting. His seconds were pouring water on him, begging him to get up. Only the clanging of the bell as the referee reached eight saved

Johnson in 1907, the year that he cleared a path to the world heavyweight championship.

strange Joe Grim from the ignominy of a knockout.

Johnson found far sterner stuff in the demiworld of black boxing. Most notably, and most often, he fought Joe Jeannette. In 1905 and 1906, they confronted one another eight times, Jeannette winning twice, Johnson winning twice, the four other bouts being draws. Good friends, they toured the East together and got to know one another's style so well that their fights appeared to be choreographed.

Only once did Johnson battle the great Sam Langford, generally regarded as the finest boxer in the history of the sport never to be a champion. Such was his talent that years later, when he was all but blind, champions still ducked his requests for a match. On April 26, 1906, Johnson and Langford, the foremost black heavyweights of the early 20th century, met in the ring at Chelsea, Massachusetts. The fight lasted 15 rounds, and Johnson won easily. "He handed me the only real beating I ever took," Langford said. "I'll take my hat off to Johnson for that victory."

That is all Johnson would see Langford do. He steered clear of Langford for the rest of his career, and their rivalry degenerated into contempt. "They hated one another like rat poison," recalled Gunboat Smith, a fighter of the same era. Smith remembered when Johnson, in his big car, happened by Langford along the road: "He took the wheel and he threw dirt right in Langford's face. If Sam Langford had a gun, he'd a killed him right there."

Spending these years on the black circuit, Johnson might be forgiven for thinking he was just treading water, fighting for peanuts while whites hit the big time. But by 1906 the big time—the heavyweight championship itself—was a shambles. Jim Jeffries was no longer champion, and no one seemed to care who was. Suddenly, Jack Johnson had a shot at the greatest show on earth.

4
THE CHAMPION

"When I had attained distinction as a boxer and was enjoying the acclaim accorded celebrities," Johnson wrote in his autobiography, "I found that there was much bitterness mixed with the sweetness of triumph. When prejudiced and vindictive persons and organizations began pouring their wrath upon me, and I found myself beset on every side by unjust condemnation and accusations, I sometimes wondered if there was a God."

SHORTLY AFTER JACK Johnson won the black championship, he issued a challenge to Jim Jeffries, the reigning heavyweight. Jeffries replied quickly. "When there are no white men left to fight, I will quit the business," he said. "I am determined not to take a chance of losing the championship to a negro."

Jeffries did not have to fight Johnson or anyone else. The reputation of the California Grizzly as the strongest man in the world was unassailable. One story had it that the champion, stricken with pneumonia, consumed as a cure a half case of whiskey a day. "If an ordinary man took even one-third the dose of this drug you are taking regularly, James," said his doctor, "he would die." The physician warned Jeffries that even if the inspired cure worked, the aftereffects of pneumonia would spell the end of his ring career. A while later, the amazed doctor examined the champion, now fit as a fiddle, showing no sign of having been ill. "I still don't believe it," he muttered. "You are simply not human, Jeffries."

Jeffries was all too human when it came to getting tired of prizefighting—he had once broken both hands during a fight—and of realizing he stood little chance of collecting a big purse anytime soon. On May 13, 1905, he retired, undefeated, to his California alfalfa farm.

Jeffries provided for a successor, arranging and promising to referee a bout between two contenders

Unbeaten heavyweight champion Jim Jeffries (shown here with his wife) retired from the ring in May 1905, after he had defeated all the top white contenders and refused to take on any of the leading black challengers. His insistence on battling only whites was aped by the boxers who succeeded him.

he selected himself, Marvin Hart and Jack Root. (Naturally, he gave no thought to including Johnson in the elimination event.) On Independence Day, 1905, before a slim crowd of 5,000 rather bored spectators, Hart knocked Root out in the 12th round, and referee Jeffries raised Hart's hand in triumph.

This was the same Marvin Hart whom Johnson had cut to ribbons a few months earlier—the same man who had been rescued by the referee's controversial decision, the same dull, awkward fighter who holds the distinction of being the only champion in ring history never to have had a nickname. Perhaps he would have gotten one had he stayed around longer, but in his first title defense Hart had the tough luck of running into little Tommy Burns, a careful, deceptively powerful fighter. In February 1906, Burns outfought Hart, and Jeffries, again the third man in the ring, declared Burns the winner and new champion. Knowing precisely where he stood in boxing, Marvin Hart joined the Louisville police force.

Through this year of turmoil—Jeffries's retirement, Hart's brief championship, Burns's rise from nowhere—Johnson seethed. With good cause. He was black, and because of that he was left out. Race, and race alone, explained why he was fighting Joe Jeannette every time he turned around and climbing into the ring against oddities like Joe Grim while the championship was passing from one second-rate white to another.

Johnson relieved some of his frustration in the ring. Against several white fighters, he dropped his usual defensive style and aggressively tried to do as much damage as he could.

Getting mad was not enough. He wanted to get even. He wanted the heavyweight championship.

Although the odds were still against a black getting a shot at the title, they were not quite so long as before. By early 1907, Johnson actually had a few things in his favor. The first was Sam Fitzpatrick, his new manager. For several years, Johnson had managed himself, and that had been a mistake. He lacked the connections necessary to secure bouts with top-flight competition. A short, wiry old pro, Fitzpatrick had connections to burn, and, appreciating both Johnson's stellar talent and the prospect of making big money with it, he began pulling strings and making deals on his fighter's behalf.

The best news for Johnson, though, was that Tommy Burns held the title. At 5 feet 7 inches and 175 pounds—the smallest champion in history—Burns, both literally and figuratively, stood in the shadows of his predecessors. Since the days of John L. Sullivan, millions had assumed the heavyweight champion to be the greatest man in the world. When the Boston Strongboy paid his daily call at the saloon, crowds of men pressed close to shake his hand, and for the rest of their lives they proclaimed, "Shake the hand that shook the hand of the great John L."

By comparison, Burns, a Canadian whose real name was Noah Brusso, was virtually anonymous. He may have resembled Napoleon, but there was nothing in the least imperial about him. Not unpopular, he was simply ignored.

It was all Johnson could have asked for—a lackluster champion, unaccepted by the public, who somehow had to prove himself worthy of the title that was suddenly his. Given this state of affairs, Burns might be goaded into crossing the color line to face Johnson, whose credentials as a fighter few seriously questioned.

Seeing the chance of their lives, Johnson and Fitzpatrick started pursuing Burns. Reasoning that his fighter needed an international reputation, Fitzpatrick led Johnson off to Australia in early 1907. Johnson caused his usual sensation, casually knocking out two outclassed opponents and, away from the ring, having a wonderful, and very public, time with various white actresses.

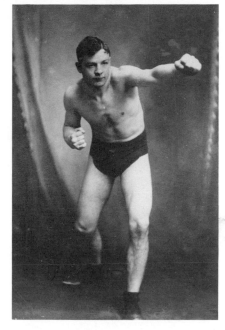

On July 4, 1905, two months after Jim Jeffries relinquished his heavyweight crown, Marvin Hart (above) knocked out Jack Root to become the world's fifth heavyweight champion. Johnson was denied a shot at the title even though he had pummeled Hart during their 20-round bout less than 4 months earlier.

Johnson, in Auckland, New Zealand, takes a momentary respite from his pursuit of 1907 heavyweight titleholder Tommy Burns. "I struggled diligently in backing up my contentions and I fought in many hard ring events," Johnson said of his boxing career up to that point. "I took on every potential contender between myself and the champion. I virtually had to mow my way to Burns."

The Australian excursion added little to Johnson's reputation. Better fortune greeted him back home, when he landed a fight with Bob Fitzsimmons, the former heavyweight champion. All Fitzsimmons had left was his famous name. Forty-four years old and flat broke, he was slow, overweight, and had lost most of his punching power. Yet Ruby Robert, as he was known, had once walked with the giants of his profession. (He remains the only man to have won the middleweight, light-heavyweight, and heavyweight titles.) By fighting him, Johnson gained a certain fame and legitimacy, and both contestants pocketed handsome purses, something Fitzsimmons in particular desperately needed.

On the sultry summer evening of July 17, 1907, Johnson and Fitzsimmons fought in Philadelphia. In the first round, both fighters gingerly circled the ring; the lack of action, in the eyes of a local reporter, was "about as exciting as a crocheting match at an old ladies' home." In the second round, Johnson let loose, and the proud old champion took a terrible beating. A right to the chin put Fitzsimmons on his back. At the count of four, he attempted to rise but fell again, this time facedown. At nine, he tried once more, lost his balance, and sank to the canvas. The fight was over. "I do not take much credit to myself for this bout," Johnson said later, "but it seemed necessary at the time in clearing the course that was before me."

Not much, or at least not many fighters, remained in the course between Johnson and Burns. What ones there were he disposed of quickly. In late August 1907, at a cramped arena in Reading, Pennsylvania, he knocked out Kid Cutler fewer than two minutes into the fight. Cutler was a protégé of John L. Sullivan. The old Hercules had made some nasty remarks about blacks in general and, in particular, predicted his fighter would "chase Jack Johnson out of the ring." With Cutler sprawled on the canvas, Johnson turned to the shocked Sullivan, sitting at ringside. "How do you like that, Cap'n John?" he asked.

On November 2, 1907, Johnson fought Fireman Jim Flynn, a white noted for dirty tactics, especially a fondness for head butts. Flynn wanted to go up against Johnson. The white fighter figured a victory would ensure him a rematch with Burns, to whom he had lost the year before. Held in San Francisco and scheduled for 45 rounds, the Flynn-Johnson fight would determine who was the number one contender for Burns's title. Johnson knocked out Flynn in the 11th round.

Now there could be no denying Johnson's right to a fight with Burns. Even the color line was getting to look like a pretty lame excuse. Newspapers around the country started an editorial drumbeat for a Burns-Johnson fight. "It is up to Tommy Burns to heed the call of the fight fans," said the St. Louis *Post-Dispatch*. "They demand that he get out of his hiding and set at rest for all time the matter of fistic supremacy between him and Johnson, between the white race and the colored."

Where was Burns, anyway? Hearing Johnson's footsteps, the champion had decided to place an ocean between himself and his nemesis. During the fall, winter, and spring of 1907–1908, he toured Europe, knocking out the English champion before the customary white-tie crowd at the National Sporting Club in London, the Irish champion on St. Patrick's Day in Dublin, and the South African and Australian champions in Paris. He was fighting everyone but Johnson, or so it seemed.

Johnson bided his time for a while, in early 1908 going on tour with a vaudeville company. His act consisted of a little boxing, a little singing, a little dancing, and, as a grand finale, playing a few tunes on a bass fiddle. His performing talents were limited, but the audiences in the little towns of the American West and Midwest did not seem to mind. They paid

Unlike most top-ranked whites in 1907, Fireman Jim Flynn (center) believed he would be granted a title bout if he defeated Johnson. But when the two men fought in San Francisco on November 2, Johnson knocked Flynn out (and did it again in Las Vegas, New Mexico, four and a half years later).

to see up close the black giant who had the look of a champion.

Johnson got back on Burns's trail soon enough, sailing for England with Fitzpatrick in the spring. There he twice fought and twice knocked out local talent. The second of the matches, against Ben Taylor, was more an adventure than it should have been. The nightlife in England, as it did everywhere, appealed to Johnson, and prior to the fight he had been drinking for several days. Not entirely sober, he managed only a wobbly performance against Taylor, luckily landing a knockout punch when his foe dropped his guard. Afterward, in the dressing room, the hungover Johnson pleaded for "an egg beaten up in a bucket of stout and champagne" as the only treatment for his throbbing head.

The English, by and large, appreciated Johnson's boxing skill and depreciated his demeanor and race. "With money in his pocket and physical triumph over white men in his heart," fumed a British boxing authority, "he displayed all the gross and overbearing insolence which makes what we call the buck nigger insufferable." Had he needed to know, Johnson was discovering that racial prejudice extended far beyond the borders of the United States.

The pressure of Johnson's pursuit was getting to Burns, and the champion started making silly claims, along the lines of "All coons are yellow," "Jack's got a yellow streak," and "I'll fight him and whip him as sure as my name is Tommy Burns." Not surprisingly, these boasts and opinions were called over his shoulder as he fled Europe and Johnson for Australia.

Johnson followed, and there he caught him.

Actually, Burns surrendered voluntarily—for a price. In England, he had agreed to fight Johnson for a purse of $30,000, but the parsimonious sportsmen of London offered only $1,500 to each contestant. In Australia, it was a different story. Hugh D. ("Huge Deal") McIntosh, an unorthodox entrepreneur who had begun his career as a pie salesman, met Burns's demand without batting an eye. He cabled Johnson, still in Europe, an offer for $5,000, which he of course instantly accepted. At long last, the Johnson-Burns fight was on.

"How does Burns want it?" Johnson hospitably asked when he landed in Perth. "Does he want it fast and willing? I'm his man in that case. Does he want it flat-footed? Goodness, if he does, why I'm his man again. Anything to suit; but fast or slow, I'm going to win."

For all his bravado, Johnson worried the deck might be stacked against him. For one thing, Australia harbored a virulent racism. "Citizens who have never prayed before," boomed a Sydney newspaper, "are supplicating Providence to give the white man a strong right arm with which to belt the coon into oblivion." In such a climate, Burns had overnight become a national hero and Johnson a black villain. Then there was McIntosh, who was to be the referee. Johnson worried he was in league with Burns. "How do you do, Mr. McIntosh?" Johnson sneered at the promoter one day. "How do you drag yourself away from Tommy?" The two nearly came to blows.

But Johnson was in Australia to fight Burns, not McIntosh, and their event took place on the day after Christmas, 1908, in Rushcutter's Bay, a suburb of Sydney. McIntosh had built a special wooden stadium seating 20,000. On the day of the fight, every seat was filled, and twice that number milled around outside the gates. It was quite clearly the biggest thing ever to happen in Sydney.

This time there were no pink pajamas for the challenger. He entered the ring wearing a demure gray robe. When he peeled it off, the crowd got its first good head-to-toe look at Jack Johnson. He was 30 years old and in the best condition of his life. Now well over 200 pounds, he carried his weight easily. The muscles in his arms and legs rippled as he moved. His head had been cleanly shaven, and when he smiled or talked, which was often, he revealed twin rows of gold-capped teeth. He bowed to the crowd and threw kisses with exaggerated gestures. The throng responded with lusty boos and calls of "nigger" and "coon."

Burns had been up late with his friends the night before, singing for them chorus after chorus of "Where the River Shannon Flows," acting as if he did not have a care in the world. The next day, he wore a blue serge suit into the ring and, like a man getting ready for bed, removed it piece by piece, methodically folding his coat, vest, and trousers into a little wicker suitcase. He was the picture of confidence. It was not so much that the Australian odds makers had made him a 7–4 favorite or that the crowd at Rushcutter's Bay was all in his favor; it was that in his heart of hearts he knew, absolutely knew, he could never lose to a black man.

At one in the afternoon, under a leaden sky, the gong sounded, the fighters sprang toward one another, and at nearly the same moment, it was plain that Burns did not have a hope in heaven of beating Jack Johnson. When he dived in and threw a left, Johnson feinted with his own left, then delivered a right uppercut to the champion's chin. The same punch that had terrorized the bully boys of Galveston now threw Burns up into the air and down onto his back. As he landed, his head struck the canvas with a thud heard in the back rows of the stadium. At the count of eight, he got up.

A portion of the noted writer Jack London's newspaper account of the heavyweight championship bout between Johnson and Tommy Burns. Johnson won the fight, which was held on December 26, 1908, in Sydney, Australia, with a 14th-round knockout.

Jack London Says Johnson Made a Noise Like a Lullaby with His Fists as He Tucked Burns in His Little Crib in Sleepy Hollow, with a Laugh

Plucky, but Absolutely Helpless, the White Man Seemed To Be the Victim of a Playful Ethiopian Who Did Just as He Would.

NEGRO'S GOLDEN SMILE A TAUNT FOR HIS OPPONENT ALL THE TIME

Smashed to the Floor in the First Round, the Canadian Fighter Was Going Uphill Ever After and Never Had the Ghost of a Chance for Victory.

SHOULD HAVE ENDED IN THIRTEENTH ROUND

Writer for the Herald Says in This Stage of the Fight Burns Ought To Have Been Knocked Out and Johnson Should Have Stopped Him Then.

WHITE MAN HITS NEGRO WHERE THE LATTER INDICATES

Burlesquing the English Accent of His Opponent, the Laughing Black Man Tells Him to Land Blows Here and There, and the Vanquished Man, Dazed, Does So.

By Jack London.

[Copyright, 1908, by the New York Herald Company—All Rights Reserved.]

[SPECIAL DESPATCH TO THE HERALD VIA COMMERCIAL CABLE COMPANY'S SYSTEM.]

SYDNEY, Australia, Saturday.

As soon as Burns was on his feet, Johnson began taunting him. "Poor little Tommy," he said. "Who told you you were a fighter?" In later years, Burns became a lay preacher, but in his fighting days he had a notably foul mouth. Goaded by Johnson, he replied with what slurs he could think of. During the next 13 rounds, his tongue did more damage than his fists.

In complete charge, Johnson chose to make a long afternoon of it. He could have finished off Burns in the first round, but he felt like prolonging the champion's agony. Round after round, Johnson stung Burns with his jab. Not aiming for a knockout—at least not yet—he wanted to punish Burns for all the insults, all the slights, all the hurt the black fighter had endured. By the middle rounds, blood was pouring down Burns's face and was spotting the canvas. His eyes were nearly swollen shut. His mouth, however, worked fine. "Come on and fight, nigger," he yelled. "Fight like a white man."

"Let's fight, you yellow gray man!" Johnson called back. "You been runnin' away from me long enough. Now I caught you. Show me if you got any guts."

Burns had guts, if little else, and kept swinging. And Johnson kept poking fun at his harmless punches. "Is that all the better you can do, Tommy?" he asked, grinning. "Come on, Tommy, can you hit harder than that?" As the rounds passed, Johnson's golden smile got broader. "Poor, poor Tommy. Who taught you to hit? Your mother? You a woman?"

After the 13th round, several Sydney policemen entered the ring and tried to talk Burns into quitting before he got hurt too badly. Burns refused point-blank. In the 14th round, as if on cue, Johnson went to work, unleashing a wicked right cross that slammed Burns to the canvas. The champion tottered to his feet at the count of eight, but the police swarmed over him and ordered the fight stopped. Restrained by the bluecoats, Burns was still breathing fire, screaming at Johnson, demanding their fight continue.

Burns's seconds led him away, and, alone in the center stage, beaming and triumphant, was the new heavyweight champion of the world, Jack Johnson.

It took a while for it to settle in: A black man was champion. John L. Sullivan blamed the greedy Burns for letting it happen. "Shame on the money mad champion!" he thundered. "Shame on the man who upsets good American precedents because there are Dollars, Dollars, Dollars in it." (Burns later blew his big $30,000 purse at the Sydney racetracks.)

When word of Johnson's improbable victory was flashed back across the Pacific, American blacks took heart. A black newspaper, without a trace of hyperbole, announced that "no event in forty years has given more genuine satisfaction to the colored people of this country than has the signal victory of Jack Johnson."

The most ominous acknowledgment of Johnson's championship was written moments after the fight by Jack London, one of America's most widely read novelists, who was covering the battle for the *New York Herald*. His story, when syndicated, was read from coast to coast. He began with a most accurate characterization: "The fight! There was no fight! No Armenian massacre could compare to the hopeless slaughter that took place in Sydney stadium. The fight, if fight it might be called, was like that between a pygmy and a colossus."

He concluded with an appeal. A dedicated socialist and reformer, London could not bear the thought of a black champion. Something had to be done, and London knew just the man to do it. "But one thing now remains," he wrote. "Jim Jeffries must now emerge from his Alfalfa farm and remove that golden smile from Jack Johnson's face.

"Jeff, it's up to you. The White Man must be rescued."

5

WHITE HOPES

WHEN THE NEW heavyweight champion of the world departed from Australia, he went to Victoria, British Columbia. Insisting on the best, he sought accommodation at the St. Francis Hotel, the finest in town. The hotel's manager politely, if firmly, told Jack Johnson to go away. The St. Francis was for whites only. Johnson smiled, shrugged off the rebuff, and headed for the second-best hotel, then for the third, the fourth, and the fifth. The managers at each place sniffed that it was too bad, but no blacks. Finally, he found his hotel—a dingy fleabag on the wrong side of the tracks.

Moving to a slightly warmer welcome in Vancouver, Johnson defended his title for the first time on March 10, 1909. More an exhibition than anything else, he took on a burly 26-year-old fighter from Tacoma, Washington, by the name of Victor McLaglen. "I outboxed Jack Johnson with ease," McLaglen recalled years later in Hollywood. By that time, he had become an Academy Award–winning movie star and, as head of a casual militia called McLaglen's California Light Horse Troop, the film community's leading fascist. In truth, during the first round of their bout, Johnson slugged McLaglen's stomach so hard that the fight went out of the challenger. For the next five rounds, Johnson joked with the crowd and toyed with the hapless McLaglen.

Jim Jeffries (left), billed as the undefeated champion, came out of retirement in 1910 to reclaim the heavyweight title from Johnson in a fight held on the Fourth of July. According to Johnson, "The fight meant more than any that had ever taken place among heavyweights."

If he had liked, McLaglen could have correctly claimed the honor of being the first of the "great white hopes," the long parade of white heavyweights set on stripping Johnson of his title and reclaiming Caucasian honor.

As the white hopes jostled for a shot at the champion, Johnson traveled to Chicago, where he hoped to enjoy his fame and spend his fortune. For several years, he had been going with Hattie McLay, a prostitute he had met in New York. She had helped finance his trip to England and had accompanied him to Australia, but in Chicago, according to Johnson, they quarreled over "her constant beer drinking." Embarrassed by her guzzling, he tried to keep beer from her. To no avail. "One day I found numerous empty bottles hidden under her mattress which attracted my attention because of the bulging appearance of the bed," he sadly remembered. They broke up, but not for good. She continued paying him occasional visits until 1911.

Johnson worried less about his own behavior. In Chicago, he lived as if there were no tomorrow, carousing until all hours, seldom getting to bed before dawn. Naturally, he bought a wonderful new car, a Thomas Flyer, the marque immortalized by its victory in motoring's longest race, New York to Paris, in 1908. He promptly wrecked it.

Following the Burns fight, Johnson had broken with Sam Fitzpatrick. In Chicago, George Little, a friendly brothel owner, began assuming certain managerial duties. These evidently included gaining entrance for Johnson to the 3-story, 51-room house at 2131 South Dearborn Street, the home and business address of the Everleigh sisters, proprietors of perhaps the grandest bordello in North America. The aristocratic sisters, however, were dyed-in-the-wool southerners and would not permit a black customer. So Little and Johnson settled for the next best thing:

They bribed three of the Everleigh girls to join them at their hotel. One was a slender, dark-complected young woman with bleached blond hair. Her name was Belle Schreiber, and that evening, she and the champion began a fateful romance.

The high life rapidly depleted Johnson's bank account. Needing cash, he returned to the ring; between May and September 1909, he took on three white hopes, Philadelphia Jack O'Brien, Tony Ross, and Al Kaufman. Johnson won all three fights, but he took none of them very seriously. Against O'Brien, he was overweight, hung over, and frivolous. Between punches, he waved to the crowd. His winnings went for a new roadster and a big diamond ring. With Tony Ross, he actually seemed bored, and against Kaufman he exerted himself only enough to win.

There could be no loafing during Johnson's next fight. He was up against Stanley Ketchel, the middleweight champion. By common consent, Ketchel was not altogether human. "Ketchel was an exception to the human race," said a reporter who knew him well. "He was a savage. He would pound and rip his opponent's eyes, nose and mouth in a clinch. He couldn't get *enough* blood. His nickname, 'the Assassin,' fit him like a glove."

Ketchel was mean, but not very big—5 feet 9 inches and 160 pounds—and appeared to have no chance against Johnson. One of the oldest adages in boxing is that a good big man will beat a good small man every time, and Johnson had Ketchel by 40 pounds.

On October 16, 1909, Johnson and Ketchel squared off in Colma, California, not far from San Francisco. The fight was fixed—at least, fixed to the extent that the principals agreed beforehand there should be no early knockouts. Film cameras were recording the battle, and it stood to reason no one would pay to see a movie lasting only a few minutes.

Johnson breaks his fall to the canvas after being decked in the 12th round by middleweight champion Stanley Ketchel. The early action in their October 16, 1909, heavyweight tilt in Colma, California, was reportedly fixed so that future moviegoers would be guaranteed extended fight footage. Moments after Ketchel broke their pact, however, a furious Johnson unleashed his arsenal and knocked Ketchel out.

If the fight went the full 20 rounds with Johnson winning at the end, there would be lots for moviegoers to see and lots for the fighters and promoters to make in film royalties.

The bull-like Ketchel had the big crowd on his side, and, evidently overcome by their cheers, he cried as he was being introduced. In the opposite corner, Johnson wore an American flag for a belt and smiled all the time at the hostile throng, seeming to delight in their shouts and catcalls.

Through the first rounds, everything went according to plan. Johnson kept under wraps his right uppercut, the one punch that could end the fight on the spot. Able to block Ketchel's blows, Johnson steadily piled up a lead, and if not very exciting, it looked like a fight certain to go the distance.

Then, in the 12th round, Ketchel damned the fix and the cameras and tried to win the heavyweight championship. Flying at Johnson, he threw his best punch, a roundhouse right. It landed behind Johnson's ear and knocked the champion down. As he fell, he caught himself on the canvas with his outstretched left arm. He landed sitting down. Although stunned, neither his smile nor his senses deserted him. As he lumbered to his feet, Ketchel shot toward him, ready to finish the job. Furious at being double-crossed, Johnson unloaded a barrage of punches. His fabled right uppercut hit Ketchel's open mouth, broke several teeth, and sent the middleweight champion crashing to the ground, stone cold out. It took several minutes for him to come to.

There were no hard feelings. That night, the 2 fighters had a rollicking good time at a local gambling hall, and Ketchel took Johnson for $700 shooting craps. Sadly, the fight was one of Ketchel's last. A hard liver not unlike Johnson, he died a notable death. As John Lardner wrote, "Stanley Ketchel was 24 years old when he was fatally shot in the back by the common-law husband of the lady who was cooking his breakfast."

Johnson celebrated his spectacular knockout of Ketchel with a cross-country joyride. From San Francisco to Chicago, he and Belle Schreiber traveled by rail in a stately first-class compartment. From Chicago, they raced eastward in one of Johnson's big cars driven by a white chauffeur in full livery. In New York, at the Coney Island racetrack, the champion discovered a new romantic interest, Etta Terry Duryea, a handsome blond divorcée. She joined the Johnson entourage, which now included not only Belle but old flame Hattie McLay as well. Johnson masterfully juggled his time and affections. Arriving in Philadelphia, he got rooms for the three women in separate hotels and spent much of each evening going from one to the other.

Johnson did nothing to conceal his arrangements with white women nor anything to hide his drinking,

gambling, and general contempt for conventional society. In fact, he went out of his way to advertise.
Quite naturally, his flaunting of custom worked millions of whites into a fine lather and added a note of
urgency to their search for the great white hope. But
the ranks of white fighters were getting noticeably
thin. In his first year as champion, with hardly any
effort—almost between drinks—Johnson had smashed
five hopes. His slaughter of Ketchel was the last straw.
One man, and one man alone, had to come to the
rescue of white supremacy. As Jack London had announced in Australia, it was up to superman Jim
Jeffries.

At first, the former champion had no taste for a
comeback. Happily harvesting alfalfa on his California farm and tending bar in his Los Angeles saloon,
Jeffries had ballooned to well over 300 pounds and
had not laced on his boxing gloves in years. But the
endless appeals to racial pride eventually reached
him—as did the promise of becoming the richest
prizefighter in history. In late 1909, Jeffries consented
to fight Johnson as an answer, he said, to "that portion of the white race that has been looking to me
to defend its athletic superiority."

Jeffries against Johnson. Almost at once there was
excited talk about "the battle of the century." The

fight promoters of the world could see nothing but dollar signs. The managers for Johnson and Jeffries announced that the fight would be staged by the highest bidder.

In December 1909, around a table covered with plates of food and bottles of champagne at the Hotel Meyer in Hoboken, New Jersey, Johnson sat with the fight managers and with every major promoter or his representative. One by one, the envelopes containing the bids for promoting the fight were opened and announced. Each offer was enormous.

Finally, they came to the envelope submitted by a relative newcomer to the fight game, George Lewis "Tex" Rickard. When his envelope was ripped open, out spilled a written bid, a certified check for $5,000, and 15 thousand-dollar bills. Johnson's eyes widened. Rickard promised the fighters $101,000, a fifth of it then and there. The winner would receive 75 per cent.

There was more. Two-thirds of the lucrative film rights would go to Johnson and Jeffries. All told, each contestant might reasonably expect several hundred thousand dollars, a genuine fortune in the age of the free lunch and no income tax. Hearing Rickard's offer, the others folded their hands. Rickard would be the promoter.

Thirty-nine years old, with a sharp nose, thin lips and a balding pate, Tex Rickard was one of the smoothest operators around, forever grabbing attention with the big roll of thousand-dollar bills he habitually carried and frequently consulted. At one time or another, he had been a cowboy, a town marshal, and a gold prospector. Shortly after he settled down to run a gambling saloon (which his patrons swore was on the level), he began to look for something to attract more business to his place and stumbled onto boxing. In 1906, he staged a match between two top-drawer middleweights, Joe Gans and Battling Nelson.

Johnson and Jim Jeffries (opposite, third from right) are all smiles at the Hotel Meyer in Hoboken, New Jersey, as a multitude of fight promoters and sportsmen hold a bidding war for the right to stage a Johnson-Jeffries showdown. The winning offer was submitted by George Lewis "Tex" Rickard (above), whose heady terms were structured so that Johnson cleared $120,000—the best payday of his career—for his part in the deal.

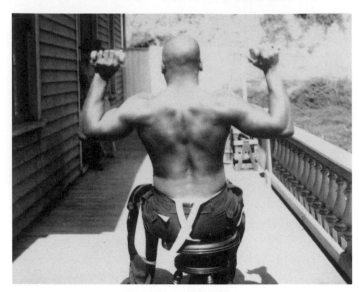

Johnson trains at the Seal Rock House in San Francisco in preparation for his 1910 fight with Jim Jeffries. The site of the bout was eventually moved from San Francisco to Reno, Nevada, after the governor of California threatened to enforce the state's anti-prize-fighting law and stop the match.

Rickard discovered that one thing about the fight added greatly to its drama—and to his gate receipts: Gans was black, and Nelson was white.

Promptly upon scheduling the Johnson-Jeffries showdown for July 4, 1910, in San Francisco, Rickard began a six-month publicity campaign that shamelessly exploited the black-white confrontation. He labeled Jeffries the "Hope of the White Race" and Johnson the "Negro's Deliverer." Not that Rickard was doing much more than adding a few logs to an already-raging fire. Millions of whites could scarcely wait for the moment Jeffries punched Johnson out. A popular song of the day, entitled "Jim-a-da-Jeff," written in a supposedly comic Italian-accented dialect, was sung with real feeling by supporters of Jeffries:

> Who give-a da Jack Jonce one-a little-a tap?
> Who make-a him take-a one big-a long nap?
> Who wipe-a da Africa off-a da map?
> It's da Jim-a-da-Jeff.
> (*Chorus*)
> Who's dat man wid-a hand like da bunch-a banan?
> It's da Jim-a-da Jeff, oh! da Jim-a-da-Jeff!

Eventually, the fighters began their training. Jeffries struggled to lose upwards of 60 pounds, and at his camp, rather than punching his sparring partners, he only tried to avoid their blows. Rickard, visiting one day, asked why he did not hit back. "I'm afraid of killing them," Jeffries explained. "My main job is getting accustomed to taking hard, smashing punches like I could years ago."

For his preparations, Johnson moved into a camp at Seal Beach along the California coast. He did some heavy work, but most of the time he relaxed on the beach, raced his car up and down nearby mountain roads, and put in regular hours at the hotel bar.

The governor of California, James J. Gillet, nearly put an end to things. Besieged by reformers up in arms about the dreadful effects of prizefighting, the governor suddenly gave in to the clamor and enforced the long-dormant California law that allowed only boxing "exhibitions." "If Tex Rickard is looking for a fight with me he will get a bigger one than advertised for the Fourth of July," said the once-supine governor. "We've had enough of prizefights and prizefight promoters."

A carnival atmosphere envelopes the town of Reno, Nevada, as the day of the Johnson-Jeffries fight draws near. Adding to the throng of die-hard fight fans were socialites and celebrities, some of the nation's most prominent outlaws, and 500 reporters.

The stage is set: On July 4, 1910, Johnson and Jim Jeffries (opposite) are introduced to the crowd on a hot afternoon in the Nevada desert. "Round about us telegraph instruments clicked off a description of the fight blow by blow," said Johnson, who as usual maintained his swaggering pose throughout the bout. "I recall that occasionally I took time during the exchange of these blows to suggest to telegraph operators what to tell their newspapers."

The state of Nevada leaped into the breach, its governor, Denver S. Dickerson, virtually pleading with Rickard to move the fight there. Rickard selected the little town of Reno and somehow in 2 weeks managed to get built a 20,000-seat stadium. Jeffries seemed upset by the change in venue, allegedly bashing his head against a wall in frustration. Johnson took it better, calmly transferring his camp to a place in the desert outside Reno.

In the days leading up to the Fourth of July, Reno became a full-fledged circus. Everyone from Payne Whitney, who left the largest estate ever appraised in the United States when he died in 1927, to Cincinnati Slim, the bank robber, showed up. Even the Sundance Kid was supposed to have been in town. Five hundred reporters covered the action from every conceivable angle. Several times that number of thieves cruised streets whose gutters were littered with the dollar watches pickpockets had lifted but then discarded as not worth fencing. All the former heavyweight champions, from Sullivan on, wandered about, each predicting a Jeffries victory. Even the black fighters Sam Langford and Joe Jeannette said Jeffries. The odds makers had the old champion a 10–6 favorite.

On July 4, 1910, a hot, brilliantly clear desert day, a crowd of thousands filed into the new stadium, checked their firearms at the gate, tried to satisfy themselves with the overpriced lemonade that was the only drink for sale, and awaited 45 rounds for the heavyweight championship of the world. For the only time in American boxing history, there were no preliminary fights. The main event was the sole event.

The crowd hissed Johnson, once more wearing the stars and stripes for a belt, and cheered hysterically when Jeffries, looking haggard and far older than his 35 years, climbed through the ropes. Acting as one of his seconds was James J. Corbett, another former champion.

"Hardly had a blow been struck when I knew that I was Jeff's master," Johnson recalled. That and more. Jeffries was helpless against Johnson. Between rounds he complained his head felt "queer" and his arms would not work right. In the second round, Johnson began talking to Jeffries and continued the one-sided conversation the rest of the way. "Don't rush, Jim," he said. "I can go on like this all afternoon." When Jeffries clinched, Johnson would say, "Now stop lovin' me like that, Mr. Jeff." And after a stinging combination of punches, "Package being delivered,

Mr. Jeff." Before long, he was looking to Jeffries's corner and jeering Corbett. "Jim," he said, "this bum can't fight any better than you could."

Once more, Johnson was delighted to let the rounds pass and draw out his opponent's humiliation. Jeffries experimented with several different stances, but "stooping or erect, he was a mark for Johnson's accurately driven blows," reported the New York *Evening World*. "Johnson simply waited for the big white man to come in and chopped his face to pieces."

The champion ended it in the 15th round. His blazing combination knocked Jeffries down and nearly out of the ring. Dazed, he staggered to his feet at the count of nine. Johnson struck him twice more on the jaw. Jeffries went down. Up again at the nine count, he was utterly defenseless. From the ringside seats,

A dazed Jim Jeffries hangs onto the ring apron after being knocked out by Johnson in the 15th round of their championship bout. In effect, Johnson's convincing victory over the world's top white heavyweight signaled the end of racial segregation in the professional boxing ranks.

people started shouting at Rickard, who was refereeing, "Stop it! Stop it! Don't let him be knocked out." Rickard ignored them. Johnson blasted Jeffries with rights and lefts, and the challenger sank to his knees for the third time. He collapsed across the lowest rope and hung out onto the ring apron. His seconds ran toward him. The fight was over.

In Chicago, on the stage of a packed theater in a black neighborhood, Tiny Johnson, Jack's mother, sat tensely, listening to an announcer read the round-by-round description of the fight as it was telegraphed from Reno. When the announcement of the champion's victory arrived, the theater exploded with wild applause. Johnson's mother smiled. "He said he'd bring home the bacon, and the honey boy has gone and did it," she beamed. 〰

6

"I AM A PRINCE.
AIN'T I?"

T HE TROUBLE BEGAN nearly at once. Across the nation, in virtually every black neighborhood, the champion's most ardent followers had been listening to telegraphic reports of the battle in Reno. At the moment Jeffries surrendered, black America erupted into fervent, prolonged, sometimes wild and drunken celebrations. As they surged into the streets, in city after city they ran headlong into embittered whites, furious at their hero's pathetic loss. The result was a national carnage.

In Roanoke, Virginia, six blacks were beaten by a white mob. In Wilmington, Delaware, a white was attacked by a crowd of blacks and slashed with a razor. In La Providence, Louisiana, two blacks walked down Main Street shouting that a black could thrash a white anytime; they were shot dead. In Little Rock, Arkansas, a group of whites and blacks got to arguing about the fight on a streetcar; when it was settled, two blacks lay dead. In St. Louis, blacks ran beside moving streetcars, jeering at the white passengers; a white, thus provoked, knifed one of the blacks.

In New York City, whites seized the offensive. "Let's lynch the first nigger we meet!" yelled one. Gangs of roving whites pulled blacks from their cars

Johnson poses with members of his vaudeville troupe outside New York's Apollo Theatre in November 1910, four months after he sent Jim Jeffries to a resounding defeat. Always the showman in the ring, Johnson equally enjoyed performing in theaters and music halls worldwide.

EIGHT KILLED IN FIGHT RIOTS

TWO NEGROES SLAIN.

Railroad Conductor and Citizen in Little Rock Kill Them in Fights.

LITTLE ROCK, Ark., July 4.—Two negroes were killed to-night by white men. One was slain by a Rock Island conductor coming into this city to-night, and the other by a man at Second and Scott Streets.

BLACKS SHOOT UP TOWN.

Kill Negro Constable When He Tries to Arrest Them.

MOUNDS, Ill., July 4.—One dead and one mortally wounded is the result of an attempt by four negroes to shoot up the town in honor of Jack Johnson's victory at Reno to-night.

A negro constable was killed when he attempted to arrest them.

HOUSTON MAN KILLS NEGRO.

Slashes Black's Throat on a Street Car After He Made Demonstration.

HOUSTON, Texas, July 4.—Disturbance broke out immediately to-night on the announcement of the Johnson victory at Reno. Three negroes were hurt by white men inside of an hour. The police were called to quell several other disturbances.

Charles Williams, a negro, was vociferous in announcing the outcome of the fight in a street car, and a white man slashed his throat from ear to ear. The negro bled almost to death before he reached a hospital.

He died later.

NEGRO SHOOTS WHITE MAN.

Assault Starts a Fight in Roanoke, in Which Six Are Hurt.

and beat them up. They set fire to the tenements of blacks and pounded on the terrified residents as they tried to flee.

In New Orleans, Baltimore, Los Angeles, Shreveport, Pueblo, and a score of other towns, the story was the same. Perhaps as many as 20 people died, and hundreds were seriously injured. Viewing the catastrophe, Tex Rickard vowed never to promote another fight between a black and a white.

The films of the fight presented an immediate problem. If telegraphic dispatches by themselves unleashed such horrible violence, what would happen when the motion picture of Johnson battering Jeffries flashed across the screens of a thousand theaters? "Decency and good order require that the public exhibition of these pictures should be prohibited," editorialized the *Independent* magazine, expressing a widely held view. Fifteen states and the District of Columbia forbade the showing of the Johnson-Jeffries film, and in numerous cities local officials blocked its exhibition. The fear of movies triggering riots did not go away. In 1912, Congress banned the interstate transportation of fight films, effectively making their showing impossible. (The law stayed on the books until 1939.)

Whether they could see his exploits on the silver screen or not, Johnson remained a hero to millions of American blacks. His reckless independence, his bold defiance of whites, his smashing of the great white hope all electrified the poor and oppressed. A street song, popular in black neighborhoods, testified to his appeal:

The Yankees hold the play,
The white man pulls the trigger,
But it makes no difference what the white man say
The world champion's still a nigger.

Leaving Reno a few days after the fight, the champion rolled across the country in his usual first-class accommodations. Arriving in Chicago, thousands of blacks greeted him like an emperor, and a formal parade carried him to the house he shared with his mother at 3344 Wabash Avenue. A few days later, he got an even larger welcome in New York. Nat Fleischer, then a boxing writer for the *New York Press*, accompanied "the Johnson Special" on its journey into the big city. "From Binghamton down to the Grand Central Station it was one grand ovation," he wrote. "When we arrived in New York City the crowd was so dense that the police could scarcely make a path for the homecoming party. The reception that Johnson received at the station was nothing compared to the giant ovation that awaited him in Herald Square when he reached Baron Wilkes' hotel. . . . Thousands blocked the parade from the station to the hotel."

Ironically, this heroic black champion redrew the color line. With Jeffries dispatched and no new Great White Hope in sight, Johnson might have at any time fought one of his old rivals Sam Langford, Joe Jeannette, or Sam McVey, the cream of the black heavyweight crop. But what was there for him to gain by fighting another black? Langford, Jeannette, and McVey were better fighters than any white, and Johnson ran a genuine risk of losing his title. Furthermore, there was not much money in it. The sporting public paid to see whites challenge Johnson; they had no interest in seeing him fight, or even lose to, another black. Being $160,000 richer for the Jeffries fight, he could easily afford to choose carefully his next opponent.

Having no one to fight did not slow Johnson down. Over the next several years, he seemed to be a man in perpetual motion. One moment he was behind the wheel of his fire-engine red Thomas Flyer, racing the legendary driver Barney Oldfield around the track at Sheepshead Bay in New York. (Oldfield

POLICE CLUB RIOTING NEGROES.

Many Fights Take Place in St. Louis Before the Blacks Give In.

ST. LOUIS, July 4.—Rioting in a negro quarter in St. Louis, at Market Street and Jefferson Avenue, followed the announcement that Jack Johnson was the victor in the Reno prizefight.

Negroes filled the streets, pushing whites from the sidewalks and insulting men and women. They seemed worked to a high pitch of excitement by the victory of their champion and to have lost all respect for the police.

Squads of patrolmen were hurried into the district and in several instances stiff fights took place between the negroes and the police.

The negroes were clubbed into order finally.

MOB BEATS NEGROES IN MACON

Many Were Arrested Also, but There Were No Serious Disturbances.

Special to The New York Times.

MACON, Ga., July 4.—The negroes here became so boisterous in celebrating the victory of Johnson over Jeffries that the authorities doubled the police force to prevent a clash of the races.

Several negroes have been beaten and scores of them arrested, but there has been no serious disturbance.

The negroes have angered the whites by insolent remarks about Jeffries.

NEGRO ATTACKED IN ATLANTA.

Streets Were Thronged Last Night, but Police Promised to Stop Trouble.

ATLANTA, Ga., July 4.—Trouble between the blacks and whites was averted to-night when the police arrested half a dozen whites and one negro.

The negro yelled "Hurrah for Johnson" on a crowded downtown street. He held a knife in his hand and in an instant several white men had struck him. The police used their clubs freely after the whites had chased the negro into an alley.

The streets are thronged with men of both races, but the police say they can prevent trouble.

A series of articles published in the New York Times *on July 5, 1910, describe the race riots throughout America that were triggered by Johnson's victory over Jim Jeffries.*

left Johnson in his dust.) The next he was in Atlantic City or San Francisco or Chicago or on tour with a vaudeville company, earning as much as $2,500 a week for his performances.

Despite the money and the acclaim, it was not a particularly happy time. On the vaudeville tours, Johnson endured racist insults and mockery. Now and then, he was made to change in a freezing alleyway or basement, separated from the white performers. In New York, he was arrested at the Gaiety Theatre, where he was performing, for assaulting a white woman. Another time, in Chicago, the punching bag he used in his act came loose from its moorings and struck a woman in the audience.

Johnson's driving habits caused endless trouble. He was arrested in New York's Times Square for reckless driving and a few days later was hauled in again, this time for parking seven feet from the curb. During the winter of 1911, he abruptly left Chicago for California. "Can't drive my automobiles in this snow," he said. "Me for the part of the country where it is warm and where I can drive those wagons of mine a mile a minute." In San Francisco, he did slightly better than that, getting arrested for driving 62 miles per hour in Golden Gate Park. The police judge threw the book at him. Denouncing the "wild, reckless racing of this defendant," he ordered Johnson to serve a 25-day sentence in the county jail. The champion did his time.

Not long after leaving the San Francisco jail, Johnson was back in New York when the police pulled him over as he slowly cruised along Broadway. His car had the wrong license plate. "I goes fast they arrests me," he said, "and now it seems like if I go slow they does the same. White man, what's the trouble now? Next thing somebody'll arrest me for bein' a brunette in a blond town."

Johnson's love life was as turbulent as his motoring. Although he kept company with an ever-chang-

Johnson's house at 3344 Wabash Avenue in Chicago, as it looked in 1910.

ing procession of white chorus girls and prostitutes, his steadiest companions remained Belle Schreiber and Etta Terry Duryea. His friendship with Belle was an on-again, off-again sort of thing. They quarreled and split up frequently but never entirely burned their bridges. In the fall of 1910, after having been separated from the champion for a while, Schreiber was down on her luck. She had lost her job at a Pittsburgh brothel. Needing money, she got in touch with Johnson. He took care of her, giving her $75, sending her to Chicago, and once there, setting her up in an apartment. In no time, Schreiber was back in the only business she knew—prostitution.

Schreiber's claims on Johnson were not so strong as Duryea's. For several years, the blond divorcée had been closest to him. At the time of the Jeffries fight, she stayed at his training camp, and the champion

Johnson drives along London's Fleet Street in July 1911. "Despite the fact that the King [George V] and his coronation were the center of attention," he said, "when my car traveled along London streets and it was announced that I was in sight, the attention of the crowds was turned upon me, and as long as I was in view the coronation ceremonies were forgotten while crowds milled and struggled for a glance at me."

habitually introduced her as "Mrs. Jack Johnson." When Johnson and his mistresses traveled together, it was Etta Terry Duryea who wore the most jewelry and stayed at the same hotel as the champion; Belle Schreiber and the others were put up across town.

But that was not enough for Etta. Having never been a prostitute, she considered herself several stations above Belle and resented every second Jack spent with her. In December 1910, Duryea's complaints evidently became too strident. Johnson exploded, swinging his fists. The heavyweight champion of the world beat his mistress so severely about the head and stomach that she required hospitalization.

The episode, for some reason, brought them closer. In late January 1911, Etta and Jack were married. The terms of their relationship, however, did not change. "He treated her like a dog," remembered another fighter.

In the spring of 1911, the newlyweds, 2 sparring partners, 2 automobiles, 1 chauffeur, 20 trunks, and a strongbox stuffed with cash and jewelry sailed for England. The champion aimed to fight Bombardier Billy Wells, the British heavyweight champion. The Johnsons arrived in London in time for the coronation of George V. "I was a bigger attraction than the king," Johnson observed. For a brief time, he may in fact have been. In the streets, Londoners crowded about him, and they thronged to the music hall to see his vaudeville show.

Johnson quickly wore out his welcome. The attitudes of British whites toward race resembled those of their American counterparts, and as in the United States, the presence of a fiercely independent, highly visible black man started rubbing whites the wrong way. The longer Johnson stayed, the less likely a fight with Wells became. "London is not Reno, and in sheer self-respect cannot tolerate this bout," said a local official. The British Empire ruled tens of millions of nonwhites, and His Majesty's government worried that the kind of violence that followed the Jeffries fight would erupt in the colonies if Johnson fought and, as seemed inevitable, beat Wells. In the end, Home Secretary Winston Churchill barred an interracial fight, and by Christmas 1912 Johnson was back in the United States.

At home, he had better luck in finding someone to fight. On July 4, 1912, he squared off against Fireman Jim Flynn, a 33-year-old white hope whom he had knocked out in November 1907. Although it had been two years since the last heavyweight championship fight, the public managed to contain its enthusiasm. In out-of-the-way Las Vegas, New Mexico, where the Johnson-Flynn rematch was held, a mere 5,000 spectators showed up, and Jack Curley, the promoter, took a financial whipping.

Flynn did not have a prayer. A veteran fighter, he had beaten several other white hopes, but he was not of championship caliber. Shortly before the fight, his trainer walked out on him. "He is hog fat and has no chance whatever with Johnson," he snorted. Still, the challenger was determined. He said he would rather die than lose and told Curley to shoot him if Johnson won.

Badly beaten through the first five rounds, Flynn changed tactics in the sixth. He started fouling. Repeatedly, he jammed his head under Johnson's chin, then began jumping up and down, butting the champion with his skull. The referee told him to stop it. Flynn kept right on. Finally, in the ninth round, the police stopped the ludicrous affair, and the referee declared Johnson the winner.

A week after the encounter with Flynn, Johnson presided over the opening of Café de Champion, his new saloon on the South Side of Chicago. "It was one of the most spectacular affairs ever held in Chicago," Johnson recalled, "and I doubt if a similar event has ever taken place anywhere in the world." As always he was overstating things a bit, but the Café de Champion was quite a place. Its rooms contained solid mahogany furniture, silver cuspidors, and, according to Johnson, "a few real Rembrandts" hung from its walls of red and gold damask. With an orchestra and dancing, a dining room and bar, the café was a hit from the beginning. No one enjoyed it more than Johnson. He led the drinking and carousing, smiled as patrons inspected the huge painting of him and Etta embracing, and late at night joined the band to sing the popular tune "I Love My Wife."

Etta Johnson never joined in on the chorus. For her, marriage had been calamitous. Jack abused her. People shunned her. She was miserable in the black neighborhoods of Chicago. "I am a white woman and tired of being a social outcast," she cried to one of her maids. "All my misery comes through marrying a black man. Even the negroes don't respect me. They hate me."

On the evening of September 11, 1912, in an upstairs room of the café, she placed several telephone calls, dismissed her two maids, and then, just as methodically, pointed the barrel of one of her husband's guns to her temple and pulled the trigger. She died several hours later in Providence Hospital.

Johnson grieved—but not for very long. Within a month of his wife's suicide, he was making the rounds with Lucille Cameron, an 18-year-old prostitute and an employee at his café. Their plainly public affair shocked nearly everyone who heard about it, including Mrs. F. Cameron-Falconet, Lucille's mother. She stormed to Chicago from her home in Minneapolis. Claiming Johnson had abducted her daughter, she demanded that federal authorities arrest the champion. The law could not oblige her fast enough. On October 18, 1912, they arrested Johnson and charged him with violating the Mann Act.

The Mann Act—formally known as the White Slave Traffic Act of 1910—had placed the federal government squarely in the battle against "the moral vice," prostitution. The Mann Act made it a crime for anyone to transport a female across state lines for an immoral purpose. Its targets were the "white slavers" who supposedly smuggled girls into the country and then hustled them east to west. But its language was so broad that any man who traveled across a state line with a woman other than his wife and then had sexual relations with her was committing a federal crime.

In practice, the Justice Department used the act selectively, principally against the operators of brothels. Individuals, regardless of their morality, were generally left alone. Federal authorities were to make an exception for Jack Johnson. They were out to get him.

The government was responding to popular sentiment. Johnson's long-standing affection for white women, Etta's suicide, and now his public affair with

Johnson's most formidable opponent began to rear its ugly head in October 1912, when federal authorities charged him with violating the Mann Act, the anti-prostitution law that made it illegal to transport a female across state lines and have sexual relations with her. The U.S. government counted on persuading 18-year-old Lucille Cameron (above), reportedly on intimate terms with the boxer, to act as its star witness against Johnson.

Lucille Cameron all combined for a poisonous public attitude. White America wanted Johnson locked up. He had gone too far.

When Johnson appeared in public, he attracted cursing mobs. "Lynch him!" they shouted. "Lynch the nigger!" A man dropped an inkwell on the champion from an upper story of the First National Bank Building in Chicago. It barely missed him. Editorial writers outdid one another in describing his shame. Even the *Police Gazette*, normally a fairly tolerant viewer of human frailty, joined the bandwagon of condemnation. The journal's sportswriter described Johnson as "the vilest, most despicable creature that lives."

But when it came to Lucille Cameron, the government had absolutely no case. She had worked in a Minneapolis brothel before meeting Johnson, had come to Chicago on her own, and had never traveled outside of Illinois with the champion. Despite considerable arm twisting, the federal attorneys could not persuade her to testify against Johnson. During her appearance before a grand jury, she broke down into hysterical tears.

The government was in real trouble. The public fully expected a prosecution. Popular anger at Johnson was growing by the day. Realizing it would be a political disaster to let him off, the Department of Justice and the Bureau of Investigation (the forerunner of the FBI, the Federal Bureau of Investigation), with the encouragement of Attorney General George Wickersham, began combing through Johnson's past, hunting for another Mann Act violation—one that would stick.

They found what they were looking for when they found Belle Schreiber. Her affair with Johnson over, perhaps feeling a little jilted, Schreiber gladly cooperated with the investigators. She had a remarkable memory. She recalled in vivid detail the names, dates, and places of her travels with Johnson. On November 7, 1912, she told her story to a federal grand jury in Chicago. The jury swiftly indicted Johnson for violating the Mann Act, and just as swiftly federal judge Kenesaw Mountain Landis, who later became the first commissioner of baseball, issued a warrant for the champion's arrest.

Federal agents went first to the Café de Champion but found it closed, its windows boarded. They soon located Johnson in room 21 of the Hotel Vendôme on State Street. Breaking down the door of his room, they pushed past the champion's bodyguards and explained their business. They allowed Johnson to telephone a bail bondsman. Then they brought out a set of handcuffs and snapped them around his wrists. Johnson started to cry.

He spent a week in jail before his $30,000 bail could be arranged. There were no more tears; his old swagger returned. "I want a dozen candles so I can have more light, a box of cigars, and a case of champagne," he demanded from his cell. He missed his valet and haughtily asked the jailer to assume certain duties, such as bending down and removing the champion's shoes. When the jailers refused all his requests, Johnson compared their place unfavorably to the one in San Francisco: "When I was in jail in California those gentlemen always treated me like a prince. And I am a prince. Ain't I?" ☙

7

EXILE

IT WAS A short ceremony, no longer than three minutes. It took place on December 4, 1912, in the parlor of the house on Wabash Avenue in Chicago. A black minister presided, and a white saloonkeeper was the best man. The bridegroom wore a muted houndstooth check suit and an unpatterned bow tie, the bride a big plumed hat with an upturned brim and a wool suit that flattered her hourglass figure. When their vows had been taken, a little band started to play, the wedding guests paired off for dancing, white-coated waiters uncorked the champagne, and the bridegroom slipped the wedding ring from his wife's finger and dropped it into his pocket for safe-keeping. Jack Johnson had married Lucille Cameron.

Tiny Johnson was present. Asked about her son's marriage, she replied, "Sometimes I say things Jack doesn't like, so I'll keep my thoughts to myself." The bride's mother was not there. "Where's your mother, Mrs. Johnson?" asked a reporter.

"I don't know and I don't care," came the reply.

She seemed to care only about her new husband. After it had become clear the government could not make a case of Johnson "abducting" Lucille, it had,

In December 1912, less than a month after he was released on bail after being arrested for violating the Mann Act, Johnson married Lucille Cameron, the woman he had allegedly compromised, in his Chicago home. The boxer's mother, Tiny (right), was among the small group that attended the ceremony.

with no legal foundation, continued to hold the young woman as a material witness in a Rockford, Illinois, penitentiary. After a while, reporters began asking why Lucille was still in jail. No formal charges of abduction, after all, had been filed against the champion. Not having much of an answer, the government released her. She rushed to Johnson and, according to him, "begged me to marry her."

If Johnson's wish was to turn the flames of the public's anger into an absolute inferno, his marrying Lucille Cameron was a masterstroke. Even black America condemned him, or at least its newspapers did. The Baltimore *Afro-American Ledger* concluded the champion had "proved himself anything but a credit to his race." The New York *Age* decided that "as a black champion he has given the Negro more trouble by his scandals than he did in twenty years as a black tramp." And the *Philadelphia Tribune* ran the blunt headline JACK JOHNSON, DANGEROUSLY ILL, VICTIM OF WHITE FEVER.

The white patriots of racial purity virtually foamed at the mouth. On the floor of the House of Representatives, Seaborn A. Roddenberry, a member from Georgia, announced, "In Chicago, white girls are made the slaves of an African brute." Unless a constitutional amendment outlawing interracial marriage were enacted, there would be another civil war. Intermarriage, Roddenberry ranted, "is destructive of moral supremacy, and ultimately this slavery of white women to black beasts will bring this nation to a conflict as fatal and as bloody as ever reddened the soil of Virginia or crimsoned the mountain paths of Pennsylvania."

Meanwhile, the government was putting the finishing touches on its case against Johnson for violations of the Mann Act. In early 1913, federal attorneys issued a formal indictment charging him with 11 counts of prostitution, debauchery, unlawful sexual intercourse, inducement of prostitution, and crimes against nature. The indictment covered a lot of territory, but the heart of the prosecution was Johnson's relations with Belle Schreiber during the fall and winter of 1910, when the champion had given her money, directed her to Chicago, and arranged an apartment for her.

"It was a rank frame up," Johnson recalled in his memoir, and for once he was not exaggerating in any way.

In its prosecution, the government bulled through the traditional protections of due process and presumption of innocence. It violated the spirit (if not the letter) of the Mann Act by pursuing somebody who had never earned a penny from prostitution. (Indeed, money for sex was never an issue; for Belle, Jack was always a nonpaying customer.) On top of that, nearly all the trips Johnson and Schreiber took together were *before* the Mann Act went into effect on July 1, 1910.

The government's case boiled down to this: Johnson sent money to Schreiber in October 1910 and transported her to Chicago solely so she could practice prostitution.

The trial began in Chicago federal court on May 7, 1913. Assistant District Attorney Harry Parkin, opening for the government, trained his artillery on Johnson. The champion, he said quietly, was a monster: "It will appear that those women who he carried about the country with him were, very, very many times, when he had a fit of anger, or when the girls refused to do some of the obscene things he demanded of them—that he practiced the manly art of self-defense upon them, blacking their eyes and sending them to hospitals."

Belle Schreiber was the star witness. Hour after hour, she recounted her life with the champion, leaving little to anyone's imagination. Her keyhole view

Belle Schreiber, one of Johnson's former lovers, was the government's chief witness against the heavyweight champion after he was arrested for violating the Mann Act. The case went to trial in May 1913 and culminated in a guilty verdict, with a federal judge sentencing Johnson to pay a $1,000 fine and spend a year and a day in prison. "The whole accusation," the boxer maintained, "was unfounded."

of life was very interesting, but because nearly all she described happened prior to the passage of the Mann Act, it was hopelessly irrelevant.

Her manner was entirely matter-of-fact. "Were you in love with him?" Johnson's attorney asked during cross-examination.

"I don't know," she said. The lawyer asked the question twice more. Finally, Schreiber said, "I don't know what love is. . . . I don't believe I ever was in love." Given her hard looks and hard life, not a soul in the courtroom doubted her answer.

Johnson took the stand in his own defense. He was neither humble nor contrite. He did not apologize once for the way he chose to live his life. He said Schreiber was an old friend to whom he had offered a helping hand. "Did you have a conversation with Belle Schreiber over the telephone in October 1910?" his lawyer asked.

"Yes," said Johnson, "she called me up and asked me to send her $75."

"When you sent the $75," his counsel asked a few minutes later, "did you have any intention she should come here for immoral purposes, collectively or individually?"

"No, I did not."

"When you came to Chicago about this time did you come here to see Belle?"

"No. I came on arrangements about some boxing."

On cross-examination, the prosecutor attempted to establish that Johnson had profited from Schreiber's business: "Didn't you forcibly take $20 from Belle Schreiber which she earned immorally?"

"No. I never took a dollar, a cent, or even a newspaper from her. What would I want with $20 when I was earning $2,500 a week?"

It was his word against the government's. In support of its brief, the government presented not a shred of documentary evidence—no telegrams, no train tickets. Nothing.

The flimsiness of the federal prosecution was lost on the 12 white jurors. A few minutes before midnight on May 13, 1913, after deliberating an hour and three-quarters, the jury filed into the courtroom. The foreman rose, cleared his throat, and said: "We, the jury, find the defendant, John Arthur Johnson, guilty as charged in the indictment."

Afterward, District Attorney Parkin admitted that not all the legal niceties had been observed. But it was something that had to be done: "This negro, in the eyes of many, had been persecuted. Perhaps as an individual he was. But it was his misfortune to be the foremost example of the evil in permitting the intermarriage of blacks and whites."

While awaiting sentencing, Johnson went about his business in a familiar way. He installed a cutout muffler on one of his cars, making the engine's already formidable sound an earsplitting roar. Day and night, the champion could be seen, and all too loudly heard, racing about Chicago.

On June 4, 1913, Federal Judge George Carpenter sentenced Johnson to pay a fine of $1,000 and to spend a year and a day in the federal penitentiary at Joliet, Illinois. The judge granted the champion two weeks to file an appeal. During that time, federal agents kept up their constant surveillance. "My car and my house were watched day and night," Johnson recalled. "Every step I took was dogged. I was haunted every minute of my life and I must admit that it got on my nerves."

He decided to escape. Believing himself innocent and rightly concluding an appeal would fail, Johnson realized that it came down to a choice between a year in prison or life abroad. Once he set foot on foreign soil, he would be safe; violations of the Mann Act were nonextraditable.

Johnson at his freest: behind the wheel of a race car. In June 1913, he made an even bolder move toward freedom when he fled to Paris to avoid serving his prison sentence.

Escape was simply accomplished. First things first, he had two of his cars, an Austin roadster and a Chalmers limousine, shipped to Europe. He purchased railway and steamship tickets from Chicago to Le Havre, France, by way of Montreal. He told anyone who would listen that he would be off for a few days of fishing in Cedar Lake, Indiana. Then, while supposedly baiting his hook, he left for Canada. From there he sailed for Europe.

But what about all the federal agents on his doorstep? They wound up looking like fools. In truth, they knew all about his escape and let him go. Johnson helped ease the way by bribing several of his shadows to look the other way. But no amount of cash could have done the job had the government been determined to see him in prison. The Justice Department apparently decided that getting Johnson out of the country served the public interest. If he went to prison, they reasoned, he would be out in a year and would probably start stirring up trouble again. If he escaped, he would be gone for good. Let Europe worry about him.

By the end of June 1913, the champion and his wife had arrived in Paris. Away from their American tormentors, the couple might have hoped to be away from racial prejudice. In certain respects, they were. The French possessed a greater tolerance than the Americans or British, and for the first time in quite a while Johnson heard the cheers of a crowd. At the Folies Bergère, a spotlight was trained on him and the performers insisted he come to the stage to take a bow. Yet, as at home, he could be slapped in the face with racist rejection. The best hotels in Paris, for instance, refused him accommodation.

Naturally, Johnson indulged in the sensual pleasures of Paris and, it was said, traveled about the city like a prince. But before long, his roll of thousand-dollar bank notes had gotten rather thin, and in France he had no way of restoring it. Largely because of his problems with the language, his vaudeville act had flopped in Paris, and French stage managers shied away from him.

Johnson turned to England. Hoping for a profitable run in the music halls of London, he got instead a very chilly reception. His trial and conviction had been big news in Britain. Other performers protested his lack of "public decency" and demanded he be barred from the stage. Newspaper editorialists and crusading ministers lent their voices to the clamor against the champion, one saying it would be a "public scandal" for him to perform.

While waiting for the storm to blow over, Johnson boxed a few exhibitions, but those ended when a drunken taxi driver smashed into his car while he and Lucille were driving near Victoria Station in London. The accident caused him to wrench his back. Soon after, with an aching back and a wrecked roadster, he dejectedly returned to Paris. He was flat broke.

Pursued by his creditors, Johnson earned what he could. In December 1913, his desperation was such that he broke his self-established color line and fought another black, "Battling" Jim Johnson. A comparative unknown, Jim Johnson was no threat to win the title, but in the course of the 10-round fight, the champion broke the radius bone in his left arm. In severe pain, Johnson fought even more defensively than usual. His strategy displeased the crowd. They first shouted for "action," then started yelling "fake," and when Jack Johnson's victory by decision was proclaimed, they screamed for "our money back." For the evening's work, the champion collected 35 percent of the $3,000 gate.

One thousand fifty dollars was dust in the balance to what he needed. So Johnson tried wrestling, giving a series of performances at the Nouveau Cirque in Paris. He also wrestled for private viewers. In early 1914, he told Dan McKetrick, the leading promoter of boxing in Paris, he was going to Germany for a wrestling match at the estate of a Hamburg brewer.

"Wrestling for brewers!" McKetrick shouted. "You might get killed."

"I'm needy," Johnson pointed out. It worked well; he was paid in cash, and the brewer let him have all the beer he wanted.

McKetrick arranged Johnson's best chance for a good payday when he promoted a championship fight with Frank Moran. A former sailor from Pittsburgh who had once served on the presidential yacht during Theodore Roosevelt's administration, Moran was a respectable white hope, if no world beater. That was fine with Johnson. Broke and in exile, the champion was not really interested in getting into the fight of his life. He wanted to make some money, not risk his title.

The fight was held on June 27, 1914, at the Vélodrome d'Hiver, a Paris bicycle track. It was a long way from Reno. A canopy of purple silk hung above the ring. In white tie and bejeweled gowns, some of the more celebrated men and women of Continental society coasted through the crowd of 7,000. Looking

Johnson during his self-imposed exile, with his wife Lucille, at the racetrack in Paris.

dashing in a silk shirt and white flannels was the referee, Georges Carpentier, the elegant 160-pound boxing idol of France.

"Moran fought splendidly," Johnson recalled, "and I shall always remember it as an event of more than passing importance in my ring activities." He was the only one who did. The reporter for the *New York Times* wrote, "It was positively the poorest bout ever staged as a championship contest." Moran's "Mary Ann," as he called his best punch, came nowhere near the champion. "The only time he touched Johnson," McKetrick said, "was when they shook hands before and after the fight."

It lasted 20 rounds, without a single knockdown. Johnson clearly won, but the fight had been such a bore that the spectators booed the decision.

Jaunty as ever, Johnson found numerous ways to amuse himself during his seven-year exile. He resumed his vaudeville act, put on boxing exhibitions throughout Europe, and defended his heavyweight title in France, Argentina, and Cuba.

Boxing legend has it that nobody made any money on the fight. As the story goes, McKetrick flew into a wild rage at Moran, all because the boxer refused to sign a contract. "I vowed you would never get a nickel from this fight," he told Moran. "You or anyone else, including me. I'm tying up all the profits." He then instructed his lawyer to use every legal trick to impound the purse. There went the $14,400 Johnson was to have collected. Whether a true account or not, the fact remained that Johnson was in just as bad financial shape after the fight as before.

The Johnson-Moran bout coincided with a momentous event. A half day after the boxers left the ring in Paris, the heir to the throne of Austria-Hungary, Archduke Francis Ferdinand, and his wife, Sophie, were touring the city of Sarajevo, capital of Bosnia. As they acknowledged the cheers of the crowd, Gavrilo Princip, a Serbian student, stepped toward the royal couple's Graefund Stift automobile, which was temporarily stopped because its driver had made a wrong turn. Princip pulled out a revolver and fired twice, killing the archduke and his wife. The assassinations set off a calamitous chain reaction that, by August 1914, had plunged Europe into the most horrible war in its history. ◆

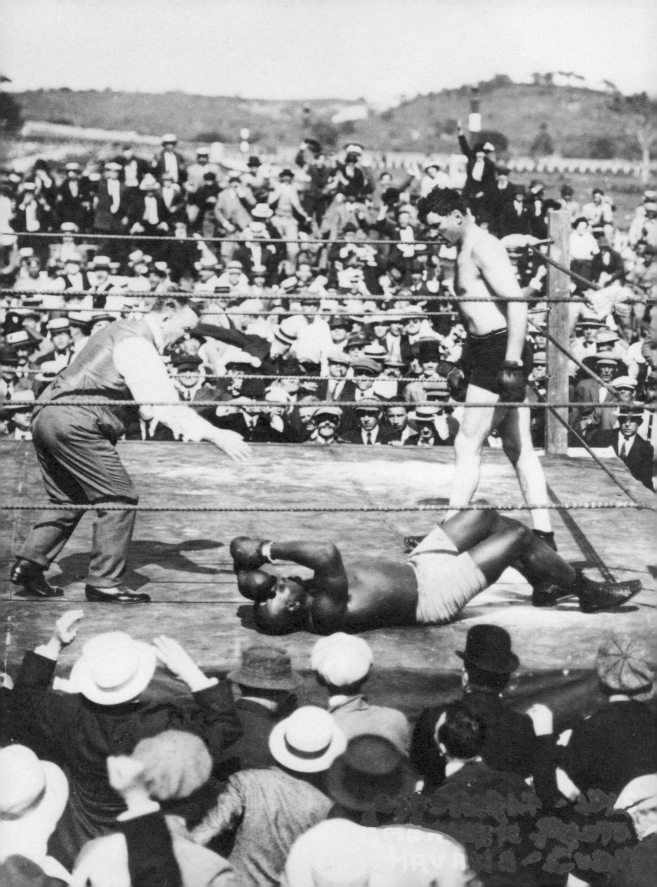

8

SURRENDER

THE HUNT FOR a great white hope was, if not very fruitful, remarkably persistent. "In the heat of the search," wrote John Lardner, "well-muscled white boys more than six feet two inches tall were not safe out of their mother's sight." They were advertised for in newspapers. They were plucked from barrooms and coal mines, rescued from farms and carnivals, delivered from shantytowns and blacksmith shops—anyplace at all where there might be found the white man who could whip Jack Johnson.

After the demise of Jim Jeffries in 1910, every fighter in the land seemed to be saying, "Why not me?" At one time or another, in no particular order, the parade of white hopes had in its front ranks Luther McCarty, Gunboat Smith, Tom Cowler, Frank Moran, Carl Morris, Arthur Pelkey, Fred Fulton, Philadelphia Jack O'Brien, Fireman Jim Flynn, Boer Rodel, Al Kaufman, Tom Kennedy, Billy Wells, Al Palzer, and Sailor White. In May 1911, at the National Sporting Club on West 44th Street in New York, there was a White Hope Tourney. Al Palzer struggled to victory. Johnson was on hand, in the front row, for Palzer's moment in the sun. "Learning anything, Jack?" asked a reporter.

Johnson's reign as heavyweight champion of the world comes to an end on April 5, 1915, in Havana, Cuba, at the hands of Jess Willard. "Preceding the fight with Willard, I did no serious training," Johnson said. "I engaged in a few boxing exhibitions and did a few 'strong man' stunts, such as pulling against horses and permitting a horse to stand on my stomach."

In the years that followed Johnson's 1910 triumph over Jim Jeffries, Georges Carpentier (above) and Arthur Pelkey (opposite) emerged as two of the leading challengers for the heavyweight title. The search for a great white hope, Johnson said later, "had been carried on so intensely and bitterly that it had caused me much trouble and sorrow, because of the persecution to which I was subjected."

"I'm learning plenty," said the champion before dissolving into uproarious laughter. A not dissimilar reaction greeted most suggestions of a Palzer-Johnson title fight. Three years later, Palzer's father killed him during a family brawl.

Something always seemed to be happening to the white hopes. Johnson, of course, took care of several himself. But the most damage was done by one to another. Carl Morris, "the Salupa Giant," bled so profusely during his fight with Fireman Flynn that the referee needed to change his shirt between rounds. Luther McCarty, perhaps the best of the lot, had the terrible misfortune of fighting once too often before he sailed to Europe for a bout with Johnson. In the first round against Arthur Pelkey, he took a light punch to the side of the head and fell to the canvas. Eight minutes later he was pronounced dead, the victim of a brain hemorrhage. Gunboat Smith, so named for the enormous size of his feet, actually made it to Europe in a halfhearted pursuit of Johnson. But once there, he lost his "white championship" to Georges Carpentier, the wasp-waisted French boxer who had refereed the Johnson-Moran fight. He lost on a foul. "They said I hit him while he was down," Smith remembered more than a half-century later. "I said, 'He wasn't down in the first place. I didn't hit him hard enough.' He ducked. That's the way he used to duck."

Carpentier, in the eyes of sportswriter Heywood Broun, possessed "one of the most beautiful bodies the prize ring has known." "Michelangelo," wrote another contemporary, "would have fainted for joy with the beauty of his profile." A match between Johnson and this dashing Adonis would have captivated Europe, but at about 160 pounds Carpentier had the good sense not to press his luck. What was more, at the beginning of the First World War he joined the French army. The "white championship" vanished with his answering the call to arms.

That made Jess Willard, "the Pottawatomie Giant," the outstanding white hope. The prospect of Willard against Johnson did not quicken many pulses. The manager of a rival fighter said Willard was "no better qualified to fight for the title than the average spermaceti whale."

"God made me a giant," Willard said. Born on a Kansas ranch, he had grown to be 6 feet 6 inches tall and to weigh more than 250 pounds. In his mid-twenties, he gave up on ranch work: "I just sat down and figured that a man as big as me ought to be able to cash in on his size and that was what started me on the road to boxing."

Willard and pugilism did not make a natural marriage. "I never really knew how to fight," he admitted. "In the fights I engaged in I never could do anything to the other fellow in the way of damage. I simply couldn't do it. Harming the other fellow seemed to be cruel, and so long as the other fellow didn't harm me much I didn't see any reason why I should hurt him.

Willard's aversion to violence showed. In one fight, he grabbed the referee and used him as protection against his opponent's blows. Before fighting Boer Rodel, another white hope, Rodel's manager hoodwinked Willard into believing his fighter had a bad heart. "You better not hit him too hard, or you'll kill him," he cautioned. Willard thoughtfully pulled his punches and stood still as a tree, making a wonderful target for the perfectly healthy Rodel.

Willard could take nearly any punch. Gunboat Smith recalled that after throwing his best, Willard's "hair wiggled a little bit. That's all. I said, 'Holy Jesus, that was my best punch. No detours, right from the floor, right on his chin.' I says, 'Wait a minute, I'll have to try that again.' I tried it again. Nothing happened."

When provoked, Willard could become a tiger. He smashed Sailor Kearns so badly that the prostrate fighter had to be dragged from the ring, and his right uppercut not only knocked out Bull Young, it killed him. Willard was actually arrested on a charge of manslaughter but was quickly exonerated.

To some, Willard was just an outsized lummox who did not know his own strength, but to Jack Curley, the promoter of the 1912 Johnson-Flynn fight, the big man was the logical challenger to the champion. By early 1915, Curley had Willard's and Johnson's agreement for a title fight later in the year.

Johnson badly needed a fight. Since his encounter with Moran in June 1914, his debts had gotten no smaller, and the war was making normal life in France impossible. By the end of August 1914, German armies were a mere 25 miles from Paris. (The French called their enemy's largest, hardest-hitting artillery piece *le Jack Johnson*.) The French counterattack at the Marne in early September saved Paris but stopped far short of defeating Germany, and the war became a grim, stalemated slaughter. Fearful he might be conscripted into the French army, Johnson left for England.

His welcome, if anything, was frostier than before. Johnson was arrested for swearing on a London street and fined $12 for obstructing traffic with his roadster. Curley's proposal of a title defense against Willard, with a guaranteed payday of $30,000, came as a godsend.

Finding a location for the fight was no easy matter. The United States was out of the question; the champion would be arrested as soon as he entered the country. Nor could warring Europe be expected to show much interest in a boxing diversion. Curley initially thought Ciudad Juárez, Mexico, just across the Texas border, would be ideal. However, the seemingly endless Mexican revolution created such instability that the fight's safety could not be assured. Finally, Curley settled on Havana, Cuba, a spot both politically tranquil and easily reached by American boxing enthusiasts. The Willard-Johnson fight was set for April 5, 1915, at the Oriental Race Track, 10 miles outside of Havana.

Johnson took his time getting there. In late 1914, he traveled from England to Argentina, where he fought two exhibitions in Buenos Aires, then to Barbados, and from there to Havana. He would have done better spending his days in the gym training. On March 31, 1915, less than a week before his meeting with Willard, Johnson celebrated his 37th birthday. In boxing, few contenders last very long beyond the age of 30. Even though he was a fantastic specimen, the champion was living on borrowed time. And, continuing to drink and carouse, he was doing nothing to extend his days in the ring. Preparing for the Willard fight, he frequently called off sparring sessions and never ran too far in his roadwork. He was unworried. "I am the best judge of my condition, and I am satisfied," he proclaimed. The night before the fight, he bet $2,500 on himself to win.

Willard, on the other hand, trained hard for six months, pushing himself into the best condition of his life. He was ready to go the distance—45 rounds—if that was what it was going to take.

On April 5, before 20,000 spectators and under a torrid early-afternoon sun, Johnson and Willard began to fight. Lucille Johnson sat at ringside. The challenger stood bolt upright, protecting himself with his extended left arm. Clearly, he wanted Johnson to take the offensive, but the champion, as ever, was waiting for his foe to make the first move. Consequently, almost nothing happened through the first 10 rounds, not even much in the way of conversation. After a brief exchange of fists, Johnson said, "I devoutly hope I didn't happen to hurt you, Jess." He also directed some carefully chosen remarks to Willard's seconds, but it was tame stuff compared to the Jeffries fight.

In the 11th round, Johnson picked up the pace, moving more, punching harder, stinging Willard over and over. He kept it up for 10 rounds, pounding Willard relentlessly. "As his terrific punches were rained on Willard," wrote Nat Fleischer, "a murmur went through the crowd that indicated a sympathy with the white man and an anxiety to see the championship come back to the Caucasian race." Johnson seemed to be doing everything but finishing him off. In point of fact, he was not inflicting much harm. After 20 rounds, a full hour of boxing, the Pottawatomie Giant, aside from a few facial cuts, looked as good as new.

Johnson, though, was fading fast. The years had caught up with him. His wind was gone; his legs were rubbery. Short of swinging an ax at Willard, he was not going to get the challenger off his feet. Nor did he possess the endurance to last another 25 rounds.

Slowly, almost reluctantly, Willard took charge. In the 25th round, he tagged the champion with a hard right to the chest. Johnson winced. Between rounds, he knew it was all over. "It don't look—too good—right now," he gasped. He told Curley to take Lucille from the arena; he did not want her to see him lose.

In the 26th round, after a minute and a half of feinting and awkward posing, Willard directed a left to Johnson's face and followed it with a right to the stomach and a left to the body. The champion dropped his guard, and Willard smashed a right to the jaw.

Years later, Willard said Johnson without question had been the greatest heavyweight in history. Then what happened in Havana? he was asked. Willard shrugged. "I hit him a good uppercut."

The punch caused the champion's knees to buckle. He fell heavily to the canvas, where he lay on his back, his legs bent at the knees. As the referee

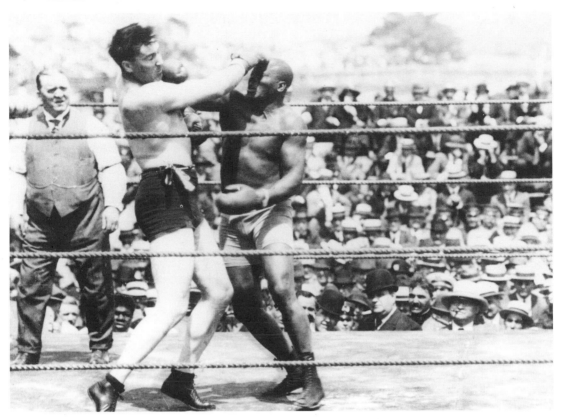

counted him out, his arm slashing the air 10 times, Jack Johnson, like a man on the beach who had forgotten his dark glasses, languidly lifted his right arm and positioned it over his eyes to shield them from the bright, hot sun.

A year or so later, that gesture became the "proof" of Johnson's argument that the fight was fixed, that he had taken a dive. Would a fighter who was really knocked out, he asked, worry about shading his eyes? He explained that he had made a deal with the agents of the federal government. In return for his deliberately losing the heavyweight title, they would reduce the sentence for his Mann Act conviction to a fine. He would be permitted to return to the United States without having to go to prison. "By the Holiness of my Maker and my dear beloved mother," he

Johnson clearly held the upper hand over Jess Willard during the middle portion of their 1915 heavyweight championship bout but began to tire in the 20th round and was knocked out by Willard 6 rounds later. Johnson subsequently claimed that he threw the fight—and his title—as part of a deal that would allow him to return to the United States without having to serve his prison term.

said, that was the truth. He he had done his part, but the government double-crossed him by leaving his sentence intact.

Actually, it was another of Johnson's tall tales. Before the fight, he had indeed tried to make a deal, but the government would not budge an inch. And after the fight, still feeling Willard's punch, he admitted defeat. "Willard was too much for me. I just didn't have it," he said to a reporter.

Willard was now the man of the hour. At the Oriental Race Track, Cuban police had to use the broadsides of their machetes to prevent overjoyed spectators from storming the ring. A few days later, making his way up the Florida peninsula, he heard "one continuous ovation." "Hey, Jess!" shouted one man. "Show us the fist that knocked out Johnson!" Willard happily waved his right hand, something "as big as a small ham." His train pulled into New York in the middle of the night. Despite the hour, thousands crowded into Pennsylvania Station to greet him, and an even larger throng paraded him to his hotel. Five years earlier, on the identical streets, the blacks of New York had hailed Jack Johnson. On the new champion's night, reported the New York *Tribune*, "not more than half a dozen Negroes were seen in the vicinity of the station all evening. The few that sauntered past got a reception that caused them to hasten their steps."

Johnson's glory days were over. No longer champion, yet still a fugitive, he once more tried England, hoping to make money showing films of his fight with Willard. Other interests, however, grabbed the movie rights, and Johnson was left with his music-hall routine. It flopped. Johnson threw a fit, slugged his manager, was sued for doing so, and had to pay more than $1,100 in damages. In February 1916, the British home secretary invoked the Aliens Restriction Act and told Johnson to be out of the country in three days.

He went to Spain, a nonbelligerent in the First World War. Taking a stab at a boxing comeback, he fought a flabby heavyweight named Arthur Craven, a poet who claimed to be the nephew of the Irish-born writer Oscar Wilde. For the remainder of the war, Johnson stayed in Spain. The American embassy in Madrid kept an eye on him for the Justice Department, but it had little to report, or at least little that was new. The former champion, wrote a military attaché in a confidential memorandum, was most often in the company of "a bunch of down-and-outs, cheap gamblers, pimps, and prostitutes."

During 1918, Johnson toured the Spanish countryside with Blink McCloskey, a mediocre heavyweight. Before each of their exhibitions, McCloskey would carefully remove his glass eye and place it in a corner of the ring. Then, and only then, would he and Johnson spar.

In March 1919, Johnson and his wife left Spain for Mexico. There the former champion enjoyed the patronage of Mexican president Venustiano Carranza, and for a while the living was easy. Johnson had a few fights, promoted several others, and in Tijuana opened a saloon, the Main Event Café. The saloon's customers heard in great detail about the proprietor's plans for a comeback, of his wish for a shot at Jack Dempsey, the new heavyweight champion. The fact that Dempsey, in the process of beating Willard, had knocked the Pottawatomie Giant down seven times in the first round did not seem to faze Johnson. He knew he could beat the reigning champ.

In May 1920, Carranza was assassinated and his government overthrown. Friends of the old regime became enemies of the new, and Johnson was no exception. The government closed his saloon, barred him from fighting, and gave him until the end of July to get out of the country.

Johnson was at the end of his rope. Miserable and deserted, he had nowhere to go but home. He tried

Johnson and his wife Lucille stand outside their Tijuana saloon, the Main Event Café, in May 1920, shortly before the collapse of the Mexican government forced them to leave the country. With no other allies to turn to, Johnson decided to end his self-imposed exile and return to the United States.

Johnson surrenders to a California sheriff on the morning of July 20, 1920, at the Mexico–United States border. The boxer agreed to give himself up to federal authorities providing that they did not handcuff him like a common criminal.

to negotiate a reduced sentence with the Bureau of Investigation but to no avail. The government still had something to prove and demanded his "unconditional surrender." As time was running out on him in Mexico, he asked a small favor. He would come home and surrender, he told a federal agent, as long as he was not handcuffed like a common criminal.

On the morning of July 20, 1920, wearing a suit that had seen better days, Johnson crossed the border to California, ending his exile. A little knot of people awaited him. He shook hands with the federal marshal, smiled for the news cameramen, and chatted to the reporters. "No man, unless he has been through the experience, can realize the relief it brings when he returns to his country after being in exile for seven years," he said. Eventually, Johnson and the marshals climbed onto a train bound for Chicago. There were no handcuffs.

The government still maintained Johnson was a dangerous white slaver, and the federal court in Chicago resentenced him to a year in prison. In the fall of 1920, he was transported to the penitentiary at Fort Leavenworth, Kansas. He was very much a celebrity. Several hundred curious Kansans greeted his train, and a black chauffeur let Johnson drive a big limousine to the prison gates.

For the next 10 months, inside "the Walls" at Fort Leavenworth, Johnson was an exemplary prisoner. For the entertainment of the inmates, he frequently put on boxing exhibitions. By happy coincidence, the Leavenworth warden turned out to be an old friend, former governor Denver S. Dickerson of Nevada, the man who had persuaded Tex Rickard to shift the Johnson-Jeffries fight to Reno. The former champion and Dickerson relived their

A new stage for Johnson, who always found a way to remain in the public eye: At age 58, he makes his operatic debut in Aida.

Johnson flashes his legendary "golden smile." As he so aptly put it, "I have had adventures that men of my race and nation have never had."

wonderful times in Reno, and the warden made Johnson's life behind bars as easy as possible. Always one to find a silver lining, Johnson concluded: "My stay in prison, cutting me off as it did from the perplexities and strife of life, gave me time to take stock of my friends and enemies. I came to the conclusion that one of my gravest errors was my flight to Europe."

On July 9, 1921, his sentence served, the authorities at Fort Leavenworth handed Johnson a five-dollar bill and set him free. In Chicago, a small crowd of people, nearly all of them black, gathered at the train station to welcome him home. They had planned to have a brass band, but it never showed up. It did not matter. "Chicago and my friends look mighty good to me with or without music," Johnson said.

New York looked even better. When Johnson arrived in Harlem, which boasted the nation's largest black community, thousands greeted him with a tumultuous display of affection. It was like old times. Johnson led the procession along 125th Street, flashing his golden smile and waving his silver-headed cane. Dressed in a black serge suit with broad white stripes and wearing a summer straw hat on his head at a sporting angle, he looked nearly as young and powerful as he had the day he beat Jim Jeffries. When he said Jack Dempsey's days as champion were numbered, the throng in Harlem roared the loudest.

For the rest of Johnson's life, there was always some applause, most of it sounded in the cheap sideshows and carnivals of American life. At a heavyweight championship fight, though, he could hear the roar of a real crowd. In the 1930s and 1940s, at the Polo Grounds or at Yankee Stadium, before the main event, he and all the other former champions would be introduced by the ring announcer. For a few seconds, the spotlight would again be on Jack Johnson, and the loyal followers of boxing—many of them, anyway—would raise a cheer. For a moment his troubles and exile were forgotten, and his perfection as a fighter was remembered.

On June 10, 1946, Johnson was on his way to such a fight—the rematch of the reigning heavyweight champion Joe Louis and Billy Conn in New York. Roaring along U.S. Highway 1, north of Raleigh, North Carolina, he lost control of his Lincoln Zephyr and crashed into a power pole. Johnson was thrown from the car. A few hours later, he died. He was 68 years old.

Not long before the champion's death, John Lardner paid a call at the Times Square museum that had become Johnson's New York stage. "He talked freely, and with a fine, romantic feeling, about his life," Lardner wrote. "Once, he paused, stared at me coldly, and said, 'Just remember, whatever you write about me, that I was a man, and a good one.' " •ᗡ•

APPENDIX: PROFESSIONAL
FIGHT RECORD

Date	Opponent	Result	Round
1897			
(unknown)	Jim Rocks	Won (by KO)	4
(unknown)	Sam Smith	Won	10
1898			
(unknown)	Reddy Bremer	Won (by KO)	3
(unknown)	Jim Cole	Won	4
(unknown)	Henry Smith	Draw	15
1899			
February 11	Jim McCormick	Won	7
March 17	Jim McCormick	Won	7
May 6	John Haynes	Lost (by KO)	5
December 16	Pat Smith	Draw	12
1900			
(unknown)	Josh Mills	Won	12
1901			
February 25	Joe Choynski	Lost (by KO)	3
March 7	John Lee	Won	15
April 12	Charley Brooks	Won (by KO)	2
May 6	Jim McCormick	Won (by KO)	2
May 28	Jim McCormick	Won (by KO)	7
June 12	Horace Miles	Won (by KO)	3
June 20	George Lawler	Won (by KO)	10
June 28	John Haynes	Draw	20
(unknown)	Willie McNeal	Won (by KO)	15
November 4	Hank Griffin	Lost	20
December 27	Hank Griffin	Draw	15
1902			
January 17	Frank Childs	Draw	6
February 7	Dan Murphy	Won (by KO)	10
February 22	Ed Johnson	Won (by KO)	4
March 7	Joe Kennedy	Won (by KO)	4
April 6	Bob White	Won	15
May 1	Jim Scanlan	Won (by KO)	7
May 16	Jack Jeffries	Won (by KO)	5
May 28	John Haynes	Won (by KO)	13
June 4	Billy Stift	Draw	10
June 20	Hank Griffin	Draw	20
September 3	Mexican Pete Everett	Won	20
October 21	Frank Childs	Won	12
October 31	George Gardner	Won	20
December 5	Fred Russell	Won	8
1903			
February 3	Denver Ed Martin	Won	20
February 27	Sam McVey	Won	20
April 16	Sandy Ferguson	Won	10
May 11	Joe Butler	Won (by KO)	3
July 31	Sandy Ferguson	No decision	6
October 27	Sam McVey	Won	20
December 11	Sandy Ferguson	Won	20

Date	Opponent	Result	Round
1904			
February 16	Black Bill	No decision	6
April 22	Sam McVey	Won (by KO)	20
June 2	Frank Childs	Won	6
October 18	Denver Ed Martin	Won (by KO)	2
1905			
March 28	Marvin Hart	Lost	20
April 25	Jim Jeffords	Won (by KO)	4
May 3	Black Bill	Won (by KO)	4
May 9	Walter Johnson	Won (by KO)	3
May 19	Joe Jeannette	No decision	6
June 26	Jack Monroe	No decision	6
July 13	Morris Harris	Won (by KO)	3
July 13	Black Bill	No decision	6
July 18	Sandy Ferguson	Won	7
July 24	Joe Grim	No decision	6
November 25	Joe Jeannette	Lost	2
December 1	Peter Jackson	Won	12
December 2	Joe Jeannette	No decision	6
1906			
January 16	Joe Jeannette	No decision	3
March 14	Joe Jeannette	Won	15
April 19	Black Bill	Won (by KO)	7
April 26	Sam Langford	Won	15
June 18	Charlie Haghey	Won (by KO)	2
September 3	Billy Dunning	Draw	10
September 20	Joe Jeannette	No decision	6
November 8	Jim Jeffords	Won	6
November 26	Joe Jeannette	Draw	10
December 9	Joe Jeannette	Won	3
1907			
February 19	Peter Felix	Won (by KO)	1
March 4	Jim Lang	Won (by KO)	9
July 17	Bob Fitzsimmons	Won (by KO)	2
August 28	Kid Cutler	Won (by KO)	1
September 12	Sailor Burke	Won	6
November 2	Fireman Jim Flynn	Won (by KO)	11
1908			
January 3	Joe Jeannette	Draw	3
June 11	Al McNamara	Won	4
July 31	Ben Taylor	Won (by KO)	8
December 26	Tommy Burns	Won (by KO)	14
1909			
March 10	Victor McLaglen	No decision	6
May 19	Jack O'Brien	No decision	6
June 30	Tony Ross	No decision	6
September 9	Al Kaufman	No decision	10
October 16	Stanley Ketchel	Won (by KO)	12
1910			
July 4	Jim Jeffries	Won (by KO)	15

Date	Opponent	Result	Round	Date	Opponent	Result	Round
1912				**1920**			
July 4	Fireman Jim Flynn	Won (by KO)	9	April 18	Bob Wilson	Won (by KO)	3
				May 17	George Roberts	Won (by KO)	3
1913				November 25	Frank Owens	Won (by KO)	6
December 19	Jim Johnson	Draw	10	November 25	Topeka Jack Johnson	Won	5
				November 30	George Owens	Won (by KO)	6
1914							
June 27	Frank Moran	Won	20	**1921**			
December 15	Jack Murray	Won (by KO)	3	April 15	Jack Townsend	Won (by KO)	6
				May 28	Joe Boykin	Won (by KO)	5
1915							
April 5	Jess Willard	Lost (by KO)	26	**1923**			
				May 6	Farmer Lodge	Won (by KO)	4
1916				May 20	Jack Thompson	No decision	15
March 10	Frank Crozier	Won	10				
July 10	Arthur Craven	Won (by KO)	1	**1924**			
				February 22	Homer Smith	Won	10
1918							
April 3	Blink McCloskey	Won	4	**1926**			
				May 2	Pat Lester	Won	15
1919				May 30	Bob Lawson	Won	8
February 12	Bill Flint	Won (by KO)	2				
April 7	Tom Cowler	Draw	10	**1928**			
June 2	Tom Cowler	Won (by KO)	12	April 16	Bearcat Wright	Lost (by KO)	5
July 4	Paul Sampson	Won (by KO)	6	May 15	Bill Hartwell	Lost (by KO)	7
August 10	Marty Cutler	Won (by KO)	4				
September 28	Captain Bo Roper	Won	10				

(Overall Record: 79-8-12)

CHRONOLOGY

—— ••• ——

1878	Born John Arthur Johnson on March 31 in Galveston, Texas
ca. 1889	Leaves public school to work full-time
1897	Wins first professional fight
1899	Loses to John "Klondike" Haynes in five rounds on May 6
1901	Loses to Joe Choynski in 3 rounds on February 25; jailed with Choynski for 24 days for violating Texas's anti-prizefighting law
1902	Beats Jack Jeffries in 5 rounds on May 16 and John "Klondike" Haynes in 13 rounds on May 28
1903	Beats Denver Ed Martin in 20 rounds on February 3 for the Negro Heavyweight Championship
1905	Loses to Marvin Hart in 20 rounds on March 28
1906	Beats Sam Langford in 15 rounds on April 26
1907	Beats Bob Fitzsimmons in two rounds on July 17
1908	Begins touring with a vaudeville company; beats Tommy Burns in 14 rounds on December 26 to win the world heavyweight title
1909	Beats Stanley Ketchel in 12 rounds on October 16
1910	Beats Jim Jeffries in 15 rounds on July 4
1911	Marries Etta Terry Duryea
1912	Opens the Café de Champion saloon in Chicago; first wife commits suicide; Johnson marries Lucille Cameron
1913	Convicted of violating the Mann Act; sentenced to pay a $1,000 fine and spend a year and a day in prison; flees the country
1915	Loses to Jess Willard in 26 rounds on April 5
1920	Returns to the United States, ending self-imposed exile; serves 10 months in the federal penitentiary at Fort Leavenworth, Kansas
1925	Marries Irene Pineau
1936	Makes operatic debut in *Aida*; begins engagements at Professor Hubert's Museum in a Broadway arcade
1946	Dies from injuries sustained during an automobile accident on June 10 near Raleigh, North Carolina

FURTHER READING

Andre, Sam, and Nat Fleischer. *A Pictorial History of Boxing*. New York: Bonanza Books, 1981.

Farr, Finis. *Black Champion: The Life and Times of Jack Johnson*. New York: Scribners, 1964.

Fleischer, Nat. *Black Dynamite: The Story of the Negro in the Prize Ring from 1782 to 1938*. New York: The Ring Athletic Library, 1939.

Gilmore, Al-Tony. *Bad Nigger: The National Impact of Jack Johnson*. Port Washington, NY: Kennikat Press, 1975.

Johnson, Jack. *Jack Johnson Is a Dandy*. New York: Chelsea House, 1969.

Lardner, John. *White Hopes and Other Tigers*. Philadelphia: Lippincott, 1951.

Lardner, Rex. *The Legendary Champions*. New York: American Heritage, 1962.

Roberts, Randy. *Papa Jack: Jack Johnson and the Era of White Hopes*. New York: Free Press, 1983.

Sammons, Jeffrey T. *Beyond the Ring: The Role of Boxing in American Society*. Urbana: University of Illinois Press, 1988.

Samuels, Charles. *The Magnificent Rube*. New York: McGraw-Hill, 1957.

Sugar, Bert Randolph. *The Ring Record Book and Boxing Encyclopedia*. New York: Ring Publishing, 1981.

Washburn, Charles. *Come into My Parlor: A Biography of the Aristocratic Everleigh Sisters of Chicago*. New York: Macmillan, 1936.

INDEX

PICTURE CREDITS

——— ✤ ———

ROBERT JAKOUBEK holds degrees in history from Indiana University and Columbia University. He is coauthor of *These United States*, an American history textbook. For Chelsea House's BLACK AMERICANS OF ACHIEVEMENT series he has also written *Joe Louis* and *Martin Luther King, Jr.*, which was selected by the National Council for the Social Studies and the Children's Book Council as one of the notable 1989 children's trade books in the field of social studies.

NATHAN IRVIN HUGGINS is W.E.B. Du Bois Professor of History and Director of the W.E.B. Du Bois Institute for Afro-American Research at Harvard University. He previously taught at Columbia University. Professor Huggins is the author of numerous books, including *Black Odyssey: The Afro-American Ordeal in Slavery*, *The Harlem Renaissance*, and *Slave and Citizen: The Life of Frederick Douglass*.